my table

my table

FOOD FOR ENTERTAINING
pete evans

MURDOCH BOOKS

my outdoor table

my indoor table

morning

lunch to dinner

desserts

drinks

I absolutely love cooking, almost as much as I love eating. That is the basic premise of this book (and, to be honest, my life). I don't know of any other trade that gives us as much pleasure as the craft of cooking. Most of us eat at least three meals a day — over a year that is about 1,000 meals, which, over a lifetime adds up to roughly 75,000 meals. That's a lot of different options for dinner.

Food is one area of our lives where we can be really adventurous and try new things. In your lifetime you might well own five to ten cars, a couple of hundred or so outfits and pairs of shoes, a handful of different homes, and visit a few different countries (I am generalising here, of course, so please don't take offence if you're an avid world traveller or committed fashionista). With food, however, the different ingredients and dishes you can cook and taste are endless. And that is why I'm adding my small contribution to the world of cookbooks with *My Table*.

This book came about because I wanted to show people what chefs (well, me anyway) cook and eat at home when they aren't cooking in their restaurants. Usually a chef's restaurant is defined by his or her cuisine — Italian, fine dining, contemporary or whatever, and a price point (a restaurateur does have to make a living somehow). So, when you visit a restaurant you are glimpsing the business the chef has constructed rather than sampling what they cook for their family at home. This book is as removed from the restaurant world as I could possibly make it (although there are a couple of dishes included for the 'serious' cook that I do make at home occasionally if someone has a particular request).

So, please be gentle… This is an honest representation of the meals I love to cook at home for friends, family and myself. (With a few recipes kindly given by friends who have created something wonderful at their own table.) Most of the dishes are served on platters to share. This is how I love to present food at home because food is all about sharing (and it's easier to plonk everything in one dish than serve it up individually to everyone). The book is also broken into two halves — inside and outside entertaining. Some food is simply calling out to being eaten and cooked outdoors in the summer months, while other dishes persuade you to gather round a table indoors on a cold afternoon. But don't take this as fixed in any way — in fact, don't take anything as fixed in this book. The joy of cooking is interpretation and adventure. I'd be happy if my book were treated more as a guide book for simple meals and stress-free entertaining. So omit or expand the recipes wherever you feel you want to. I have also included some of my favourite drinks, and do have to thank my good mate, Mark Ward, for these. He knows what I like to drink and has taught me some simple, stylish mixes that work wonders at any party. I do hope you enjoy reading and cooking from this book. If you take just a few recipes and incorporate them into your own repertoire then I will be honoured. And I'll know that this book has been well worth it.

Cheers, Pete

my outdoor table

bircher muesli

serves 4

200 g (7 oz/2 cups) rolled (porridge) oats

250 ml (9 fl oz/1 cup) milk

250 ml (9 fl oz/1 cup) apple juice

juice of 1 lemon

2 apples, coarsely grated

1 banana, chopped

125 g (4½ oz/1 cup) mixed berries (blackberries,
    blueberries, strawberries, raspberries)

3 tablespoons chopped walnuts

4 dried apricots or dried figs

3 tablespoons honey

125 g (4½ oz/½ cup) plain yoghurt

8 mint leaves

Combine the oats, milk, apple juice and lemon juice in a large bowl. Cover with plastic wrap and refrigerate overnight.

Mix the grated apple through the oat mixture, then divide among four bowls. Add the banana, berries, walnuts and dried apricots. Drizzle with the honey and yoghurt and top with mint leaves.

I don't know about you, but I love to start the day with something good in my system. For me, breakfast is the time to do the right thing by my body and there are fewer things more right for you than Bircher muesli. We eat this at home a few times a week, and my kids love it. It was named for the Swiss doctor, Maximilian Bircher-Benner, who created it back in the early 1900s. The recipe has stood the test of time and the thing I love most about it is that you can vary the ingredients to suit your own tastes and the seasonality of the fruit.

barbecued french toast with maple syrup and berries

serves 4

I love making this for the kids, so we have it at least once a week. Chilli, my elder daughter (2½ at the time of writing), cracks the eggs for me and mixes them by herself (I strain out the shells afterwards). We head out to the barbecue (or pop it into the frying pan) and in less than 5 minutes we're all enjoying one of the tastiest breakfasts ever invented. We have been serving this at The Pantry in Brighton, Victoria, for over 15 years — most people love to eat it with some crispy bacon for a hearty brunch.

4–6 free-range eggs

8 slices of bread

2 tablespoons maple syrup

8 tablespoons ricotta cheese

125 g (4½ oz/1 cup) mixed berries (blackberries, blueberries, strawberries, raspberries)

icing (confectioners') sugar, for dusting

8 mint leaves

4 tablespoons maple syrup, extra

Heat up your barbecue flatplate, if you're going to use it. Beat the eggs with 2 tablespoons of maple syrup and a pinch of sea salt. Soak each piece of bread in the egg for about 30 seconds so that it goes a bit soggy.

Drain off the excess egg and place the bread on an oiled barbecue flatplate or in a frying pan. Cook until golden on one side, then flip over and cook until golden on the other side.

Cut the French toast in half and drizzle with the extra maple syrup. Add a spoonful of ricotta, then scatter the berries over the top. Dust with icing sugar and top with mint leaves.

the best bacon and egg roll

serves 4

There is one thing that everyone loves to eat after a big night out, and that is a bacon and egg roll. This recipe takes the humble brekkie roll to another level with some simple ingredients that, when combined, make this the best bacon and egg roll in the world… well, my world anyway!

4 rashers of bacon

2 vine-ripened tomatoes, cut into 4 slices

4 free-range eggs

4 bread rolls, buttered

4 tablespoons ricotta or other cheese

4 tablespoons tomato relish or chutney

2 tablespoons tomato sauce (ketchup)

1 handful of rocket

Heat up your barbecue flatplate, if you're going to use it. Fry the bacon on the barbecue or in a frying pan. Fry the tomato slices in the bacon fat until softened a little. Fry the eggs to your liking.

Lightly toast the bread rolls. Spread the bases with ricotta and the 'lids' with the combined tomato relish and tomato sauce.

Fill the bread rolls with the rocket, tomato, bacon and egg. Season with salt and pepper, put the tops on the rolls, cut in half and devour.

smoked salmon and avocado on toast

serves 4

This is something I have for breakfast at least once a week. There is no 'chef's secret' to it — just use ripe avocado, tomatoes that taste like real tomatoes and are bursting with flavour, and some good-quality smoked salmon or ocean trout. The key is not to use too much of any ingredient so nothing dominates. I like to finish this with lots of black pepper, some sea salt, basil or coriander leaves and a splash of very good-quality extra virgin olive oil. I also add a couple of chilli flakes for heat… If you're feeling adventurous, spread some taramasalata on the bread first.

4 slices of soy and linseed bread

½ ripe avocado, mashed

4 tablespoons taramasalata (optional)

½ lemon

6–8 slices of smoked salmon or ocean trout (enough to cover each slice of toast)

8 thin slices of vine-ripened tomato

8 basil leaves

2 tablespoons extra virgin olive oil

a pinch of chilli flakes

Lightly toast the bread. Spread with the avocado. If you're using taramasalata, spread this on now as well.

Squeeze some lemon juice over and then top with the smoked salmon or trout. Add the sliced tomato and lots of freshly ground black pepper. Top with the basil leaves, extra virgin olive oil, sea salt and chilli flakes. Cut in half and serve.

carpaccio of beef

serves 4

If you happened to read my first book *Fish*, you would have noticed I have an interest in raw food… actually, it's a little more like an obsession. It started when I moved down to Melbourne from Queensland when I was 17 to finish my chef's apprenticeship. My first job was at a Melbourne institution called Mario's in Fitzroy. It was an Italian eatery well known to cater for a terrific cross-section of Melburnians, from politicians to musicians and artists. They had a simple philosophy on food — keep it simple but use great produce. One of the first dishes I tried was a carpaccio of beef with lemon and parmesan and I fell in love on the spot. I had never tried raw beef before and I couldn't believe how good it tasted. This recipe is based on the original version, famously created by Giuseppe Cipriani at Harry's bar in Venice in the 1950s.

240 g (9 oz) beef sirloin or fillet (less flavour but much leaner)
1 tablespoon extra virgin olive oil
125 g (4½ oz/½ cup) mayonnaise or aïoli (page 40)
1 teaspoon lemon juice
2 teaspoons worcestershire sauce
1 tablespoon veal stock or milk
I handful of rocket
shaved Parmigiano Reggiano
2 lemons, cut in half

Trim the beef of all fat and, with a very sharp knife, slice the beef into thin pieces. Put it in a plastic bag and bash it with a rolling pin until the pieces are very thin. Once you have thin enough pieces, arrange them on a platter and drizzle with the extra virgin olive oil.

Mix the mayonnaise with the lemon juice, worcestershire sauce, veal stock or milk. Season with sea salt and cracked black pepper.

Drizzle the dressing over the beef and season with sea salt and cracked black pepper. Scatter the rocket leaves on top, then the Parmigiano Reggiano, and serve with lemon halves.

king prawns with thai dressing

serves 4

Outdoor entertaining has to be easy, and this recipe would have to be one of the easiest. However, just because something is simple doesn't mean it can't look wonderful and taste out of this world. Here the prawn is the star, so ask your fishmonger to pick out the best cooked variety available that day… or, better still, call them a day or two beforehand and ask them to order in the best they can find. Great meals are about creating relationships with these people — they will appreciate your enthusiasm and if they deliver something fabulous you will trust them again and again. These prawns are served with a simple dressing that has its origins in Thailand, however you could serve it with just lemon juice, or a good-quality aïoli, perhaps flavoured with some harissa, saffron or chilli jam. Beef up the salad with cherry tomatoes, cucumber, capsicum, bean sprouts and noodles for a quick and healthy evening meal.

2 bird's eye red chillies, very finely sliced

1 large red Asian shallot, finely sliced

2 garlic cloves, finely chopped

½ tablespoon finely chopped peeled ginger

1 teaspoon chopped coriander (cilantro) root

1 teaspoon finely chopped lemongrass, white part only

100 ml (3½ fl oz) lime juice

75 g (2½ oz) grated palm sugar

2½ tablespoons fish sauce

600 g (1 lb 5 oz) cooked peeled prawns (about 1.2 kg/2 lb 12 oz unpeeled)

2 tablespoons chopped coriander (cilantro) leaves

2 tablespoons chopped mint leaves

1 tablespoon chopped Vietnamese mint leaves

2 tablespoons roasted chopped peanuts

Using a mortar and pestle, pound the chillies, shallot, garlic, ginger, coriander root and lemongrass. Add the lime juice and season with palm sugar and fish sauce to make a dressing with a balance of hot, sour, salty and sweet.

Mix together the prawns, dressing, chopped herbs and peanuts in a bowl. Serve on a platter.

I remember as a young teenager I used to stay at my brother Dave's apartment on the Gold Coast for the school holidays. I would surf all day and every lunchtime Dave would make us roast chicken and avocado sandwiches. They always tasted so good and I always felt great after eating them. Many years later Dave, his best mate and I opened The Pantry in Melbourne's bayside suburb of Brighton. When we were designing the menu, my brother said his famous roast chicken sandwich would have to be on it… Fifteen years later it is still the most popular item on our menu.

chicken larb salad

serves 4

My partner, Astrid, is the cook of this dish in our house. It was taught to her by a Thai lady over 10 years ago when she was living in far north Queensland. It's a classic Thai recipe that's a winner when you want to start the meal with something light but tasty. The beauty of this, apart from its simplicity and flavour (and the fact that I don't have to cook it), is its texture. The rice is fried in its raw state until it turns golden brown and then crushed with a mortar and pestle and incorporated into the most aromatic salad you can imagine. This gives the salad a great textural crunch that is quite unique. I love to eat this wrapped in fresh cabbage leaves — a Thai version of san choy bau.

2 tablespoons jasmine rice

500 g (1 lb 2 oz) boneless skinless chicken breast, minced

2 tablespoons cornflour

2 tablespoons vegetable oil

4 tablespoons lime juice

2 tablespoons fish sauce

1 small red chilli, deseeded and finely chopped

4 red Asian shallots, diced

1 large handful of coriander (cilantro) leaves, torn

1 small handful of Thai basil, leaves torn

½ bunch of spring onions (scallions) (green part only), finely sliced

1 large handful of mint leaves, torn

fresh cabbage or lettuce leaves, cucumber and green beans, to serve

Add the rice to a wok or frying pan over medium–high heat and cook, shaking the pan continuously, for about 2–3 minutes or until the rice is golden and toasted. Remove from the pan and leave to cool.

Grind the rice in a spice grinder or mortar and pestle until it has a coarse texture (not too fine).

Lightly coat the chicken in the cornflour. Wipe out the frying pan with kitchen paper and heat over medium–high heat. Add a little oil and cook the mince, stirring frequently, for 2–3 minutes until cooked and crumbly.

Stir in the lime juice, fish sauce, chilli, shallots and spring onions. Leave to cool for 1 minute.

Toss the mint, coriander, Thai basil and ground rice through the chicken mince. Taste for seasoning and serve with fresh cabbage or lettuce leaves, sliced cucumber and green beans.

'the pantry's' famous chicken and avocado sandwich

serves 4

4 boneless skinless chicken breasts (or roast chicken meat)
170 ml (5½ fl oz/⅔ cup) mayonnaise
1 tablespoon wholegrain mustard
4 slices of multigrain bread, buttered
2 avocados, halved and fanned
4 cooked rashers of bacon
4 wedges of iceberg lettuce
honey mustard dressing, right

Heat a frying pan over medium–high heat. Add a little oil and cook the chicken breasts for about 4 minutes on each side, or until golden and cooked through. Leave to cool a bit, then chop into pieces.

Mix the chicken with the mayonnaise, mustard and some salt and pepper. Spread over the bread and top with the avocado and bacon.

Serve the iceberg lettuce and the dressing on the side.

honey mustard dressing

1 teaspoon honey
1 teaspoon white vinegar
½ teaspoon wholegrain mustard
finely chopped garlic, to taste
½ sprig thyme, chopped
100 ml (3½ fl oz) olive oil

Put the honey, vinegar, mustard, garlic and thyme in a bowl. Drizzle in the olive oil while you whisk constantly. Season with salt and pepper.

The terrific thing about travelling is the food you get to eat. I think it is actually the reason many people go overseas — when you are in another country you eat at least two or three meals a day, and I don't think there is a better way to get to the heart of a place than through its cooking. Recently I took a holiday in Vietnam and had the most amazing time eating my way around the country. The best food I discovered was at the local street stalls and a dish I had a number of times was a banana flower salad; it is absolutely refreshing and so full of flavour. You could toss cooked chicken through this instead of the prawns, and if you can't find the banana flowers the dish is still great without them.

vietnamese banana flower salad

serves 4

1 large or 2 small banana flowers

2–3 small hot red chillies, finely diced

1 teaspoon grated ginger

2 garlic cloves, finely minced

2 tablespoons sugar

4 tablespoons lime juice

2 tablespoons fish sauce

100 g (3½ oz/1 cup) bean sprouts, rinsed

200 g (7 oz) cooked peeled prawns

1 green papaya, peeled and julienned

1 small cucumber, deseeded and julienned

1 long red chilli, deseeded and julienned

1 small handful of coriander (cilantro) leaves

3 red Asian shallots, finely sliced

1 small handful of Thai basil leaves

1 small handful of Vietnamese mint leaves

1 small handful of mint leaves

1 handful of unsalted peanuts, roasted and chopped

CRISPY SHALLOTS

4 French shallots, thinly sliced

500 ml (17 fl oz/2 cups) vegetable oil

Remove three or four outer layers of the banana flower until you get to the whitish part (not the purple part). Cut off the bottom core and the tip, then cut crossways into thin strips until you get to the bottom (do not use the small banana-looking fingers at the bottom of each leaf — discard them). Put the banana flower strips into some cold water with a bit of lemon or lime juice added to stop them discolouring, and leave for 10 minutes.

Using a mortar and pestle or food processor, pound or process the chilli, ginger, garlic and sugar. Add the lime juice, fish sauce and 2 tablespoons of water.

Combine the drained banana flower, bean sprouts, prawns, green papaya, cucumber, chilli, coriander leaves, Thai shallots, Thai basil and the mint leaves in a large bowl. Add the dressing, to taste.

To make the crispy shallots, put the shallots and oil in a small saucepan and heat until the shallots start to turn golden. Lift out with a slotted spoon and drain on kitchen paper.

Serve the salad on a platter, topped with toasted peanuts and crispy shallots.

smoked trout salad on betel leaves

serves 24

Sometimes I like to be a little bit extravagant… what I'm trying to say here is that I like to show off occasionally; not to anyone in particular, just my tastebuds. We have a little hut we like to visit in the Snowy Mountains about 5½ hours' drive from Sydney, and down there we catch some beautiful little rainbow trout and take them back to the hut to cook. My brother-in-law, Udo, is a master smoker of fish (see overleaf) and I always like to try something with that delicious flesh. I often take some Thai ingredients down to the hut for just such a purpose… I love to team the beautiful fish with some very sharp, sweet and hot ingredients. This recipe fits the bill perfectly and works so well with the trout. You could also use smoked eel, cooked crab meat or some deep-fried school prawns.

24 betel leaves

125 g (4½ oz/½ cup) chilli jam (page 164)

2 smoked rainbow trouts (about 400 g/14 oz flesh),
    either bought or tea-smoked (page 32–3)

2 red Asian shallots, finely sliced

2 long red chillies, deseeded and julienned

1 large handful of mint leaves, torn

3 kaffir lime leaves, julienned

1 large handful of coriander (cilantro) leaves

1 quantity nam jim dressing, right

4 tablespoons crispy shallots (page 29)

50 g (1¾ oz) trout roe or salmon roe

Wash and dry the betel leaves. Spoon a small amount of chilli jam onto the centre of each leaf.

Combine the trout with the shallot, chilli, mint, lime leaves and coriander. Dress with the nam jim.

Place a small mound of the fish salad on top of each betel leaf and then sprinkle with crispy shallots and top with fish roe.

nam jim dressing

4 red Asian shallots

2 red bird's eye chillies

2 garlic cloves

1 teaspoon chopped coriander (cilantro) root

100 ml (3½ fl oz) lime juice

75 g (2¾ oz) grated palm sugar

50 ml (1¾ fl oz) fish sauce

To make the nam jim dressing, pound the shallots, chillies, garlic and coriander root with a mortar and pestle and then add the lime juice. Season with the palm sugar and fish sauce for a balance of hot, sour, salty and sweet (keep any leftover in a screw-top jar in the fridge) and toss lightly.

smoked trout — three ways

serves 4

If you love food but have never yet smoked a trout, I think you should definitely get off your backside, head down to one of those barbecue or camping stores and buy a $40 fish smoker. They are worth their weight in gold — actually they are pretty light.

Everyone that Udo and I smoke a trout for can't believe how good it tastes compared to what you buy in a deli or fish shop. Smoke your trout outside or somewhere well ventilated — it does produce quite a bit of smoke and you probably don't want your home smelling like a camp fire. I have included three recipes here: the first is a classic brine method that is very simple and user-friendly, great for stirring through pasta or risotto; the second is a great Asian way of smoking fish, oysters or poultry (smoke chicken, duck or quail and then deep-fry it and you'll have something very special). And the third uses Udo's infamous beer, brown sugar and rock salt mixture, which imparts a sweetness that has to be tasted to be believed (just eat this on its own).

classic smoked trout

about 500 g (1 lb 2 oz/2 cups) rock salt
200 g (7 oz/1 cup) brown sugar
3 tablespoons lemon juice
12 peppercorns
1 garlic clove, crushed
2 teaspoons garlic powder
2 teaspoons onion powder
4 whole rainbow trout

Make a brine with 2 litres (70 fl oz/8 cups) of water and the salt (enough salt so that half a potato floats in the brine). Add the rest of the ingredients and place a plate on top to keep the fish submerged. Put in the fridge for a few hours.

Take out your fish and let it dry. Place on smoking racks and over the smoking wood of your choice. Cook for about 10–15 minutes, or until the fish is just cooked through and moist.

tea-smoked trout

30 g (1 oz/½ cup) oolong tea leaves

30 g (1 oz/½ cup) jasmine tea leaves

zest of 3 oranges

4 pieces of dried orange peel

180 g (6½ oz/1 cup) jasmine rice

200 g (7 oz/1 cup) brown sugar

5 star anise

1 tablespoon Sichuan peppercorns

6 pieces of cassia bark

4 whole rainbow trout

Combine all the ingredients except for the trout. Line the bottom of a wok with foil. Place the mix on the foil and place a rack over the foil. Turn on the heat to medium. When the mix starts to smoke, turn down the heat and place two trout on the rack. Cover the wok with a lid or foil and cook for about 10 minutes (make sure your exhaust hood is on full and the windows are open).

Take off the lid and remove the fish. Let it cool slightly before taking off the skin and removing the flesh. Cook the remaining trout.

udo's smoked trout

about 500 g (1 lb 2 oz/2 cups) rock salt

500 g (1 lb 2 oz/2½ cups) brown sugar

4 whole rainbow trout

**375 ml (13 fl oz/1½ cups) beer (I like to use VB
   or Coopers Pale ale)**

Combine the rock salt and brown sugar and rub all over the fish. Refrigerate for an hour or so.

Shake the fish out of the salt and wash down with the beer, then dry the fish.

Place on smoking racks and over the smoking wood of your choice. Cook for about 10–15 minutes, or until the fish is just cooked through and moist.

Take the fish out and place on a long plate. Carefully peel back the skin. This can be refrigerated and kept for up to four days... but why would you?

How good is crumbed fish? This must be one of the best recipes ever created for fish — when you coat the fillet in the cornflake crumb mix it actually seals the delicate flesh inside. So when you cook the fish it steams inside to give beautifully moist flesh with a crispy outer shell. We cook this at home at least once a fortnight as the kids love it and so do I. You can substitute prawns, scallops, chicken, lamb cutlets or veal for the fish, if you like. They all taste great.

crumbed flathead with chilli sauce

serves 4

60 g (2 oz/½ cup) plain (all-purpose) flour

2 free-range eggs, lightly beaten

50 g (1¾ oz/1 cup) cornflake crumbs

about 700 g (1 lb 9 oz) flathead fillets, skin and
   bones removed (or any firm white-fleshed fish)

125 ml (4 fl oz/½ cup) grapeseed oil

lemon wedges and chilli sauce,
   to serve

Put the flour in a shallow bowl, the egg in another and the cornflake crumbs in a third. Lightly season the fish with some sea salt, then dust lightly with flour and coat in the egg and then the cornflake crumbs, patting the crumbs on firmly.

Heat the oil in a frying pan and fry the fish for 30–45 seconds until golden and crispy, then turn over and cook for a further 30 seconds until crispy on that side.

Drain on kitchen paper and serve with lemon wedges, chilli sauce and the radicchio salad.

radicchio salad with croutons, parmesan and balsamic vinegar

serves 4

This would have to be my favourite salad to serve; it is full of flavour, looks great and makes a great complement to anything fried. The bitter leaves and acidity of the vinegar cut through any rich or oily dishes.

a few slices of white bread (I like to use sourdough)

¼ teaspoon minced garlic

1 teaspoon dijon mustard

1 tablespoon balsamic vinegar

1 tablespoon sherry or red wine vinegar

3 tablespoons extra virgin olive oil

3 heads of radicchio, halved and cored

65 g (2¼ oz/⅔ cup) grated Parmigiano Reggiano

Preheat the oven to 180°C (350°F/Gas 4). Cut the bread into 1 cm (¾ inch) cubes, spread over a baking tray and bake for 4–5 minutes until golden brown.

Whisk together the garlic, mustard, balsamic vinegar and sherry vinegar in a small bowl. Mix in the olive oil and season with salt and pepper.

Separate the radicchio leaves, making sure to discard any wilted ones, and soak them in cold water for 10 minutes. Drain and dry the leaves (if you want to keep them for a while before serving, cover with a damp tea towel and refrigerate).

Roughly chop the radicchio and toss well with the croutons, vinaigrette and a third of the parmesan. Sprinkle with the rest of the cheese before serving.

lebanese prawn and fish salad

serves 4

2 large Lebanese flatbreads

olive oil spray

1 Lebanese (short) cucumber, deseeded and
    roughly chopped

1 green or red capsicum (pepper), deseeded and
    roughly chopped

3 vine-ripened tomatoes, roughly chopped

½ red onion, thinly sliced

420 g (15 oz) tinned cannellini or butter
    beans, rinsed

1 small handful of parsley

3 tablespoons roughly chopped mint

1 small handful of coriander (cilantro) leaves

1 garlic clove

2 tablespoons lemon juice

100 ml (3½ fl oz) extra virgin olive oil, plus
    2 tablespoons, extra

200 g (7 oz) fish fillets (flathead, barramundi,
    snapper, blue eye trevalla, coral trout, tuna,
    Atlantic salmon or ocean trout)

200 g (7 oz) raw king prawns, peeled and deveined,
    leaving the tails intact

1 teaspoon sumac

Preheat the oven to 160°C (315°F/Gas 2–3). Seperate each flatbread into two, then tear into 3–4 cm (1½ inch) pieces. Spread in a single layer in a baking tray and lightly spray with oil. Bake for about 15 minutes or until golden brown and crisp.

Toss together the cucumber, capsicum, tomato, onion, beans, parsley, mint and coriander in a large bowl. Add the toasted bread.

Make a dressing by bruising the garlic clove with a heavy knife. Mix with the lemon juice and olive oil.

Coat the fish and prawns with the extra olive oil and some salt and pepper in a bowl. Pan-fry over medium heat until cooked to your liking. Flake the fish into large pieces, leave the prawns whole and add both to the salad. Remove the garlic from the dressing and pour over the salad. Sprinkle with sumac and toss well.

fried school prawns with aïoli

serves 4

The simple things in life are often the best, and I don't think you can get any simpler than this. School prawns are available all year round from the river mouths and inshore fisheries of the east coast of Australia, with peak supply from October to April. They are usually available cooked because they have a shorter shelf-life than king and tiger prawns, and you can find them uncooked frozen at the seafood markets. They are rarely deveined, and are only sometimes separated into three grades — small, medium and large. School prawns have a distinct taste that is sweeter than most other prawns. For me, schoolies are some of the best-value prawns available. They have been popping up on menus a lot lately; I think because they make a great starter or bar snack to be enjoyed with a cold beer… but why go to a restaurant when you can cook them up in a few minutes at home? Serve with a good-quality aïoli and sea salt, make sure the sun is shining and these prawns will look after the rest.

500 g (1 lb 2 oz) raw school prawns

tapioca flour, for dusting

1 litre (35 fl oz/4 cups) vegetable or cottonseed oil

a pinch of chilli flakes

2 tablespoons chopped parsley

1 lemon, cut into quarters

aïoli

4 egg yolks

2 teaspoons dijon mustard

2 tablespoons white wine vinegar

2 tablespoons lemon juice

6 garlic cloves, roasted and finely chopped

200 ml (7 fl oz) olive oil

200 ml (7 fl oz) vegetable oil

To make the aïoli, blend the egg yolks, mustard, vinegar, lemon juice, garlic and some sea salt with a hand blender. As you blend, slowly pour in the oil until the aïoli is creamy. Season with salt and pepper.

Coat the prawns with the flour and shake off any excess. Cook in batches in a deep fryer at 185°C (350°F) for about 1–2 minutes, or until golden and crisp. Drain on kitchen paper and transfer to a bowl.

Add the chilli flakes, parsley and some sea salt and gently toss. Arrange on a serving plate with the lemon wedges and some of the aïoli for dipping (the rest of the aïoli can be stored in the fridge in a sealed sterilised jar, as you would store mayonnaise).

If you have been to a farmers' market or visited a festival lately you may have the noticed the queues that come from one stall in particular… the gozleme stall. These delicious Turkish-style filled 'pizzas' are one of my all-time favourite fast foods, and I love watching them being rolled out by the ladies in their white uniforms and hair nets. There are a few classic fillings such as spinach and cheese, and my favourite: meat and spinach. The thing to remember when cooking is to get them golden brown (with a couple of black bits for extra flavour) and then smother them in fresh lemon juice. The kids love them, too. I reckon the first person to franchise these things is going to make a fortune (any investors out there who want to back me?)

gozleme of lamb, mint, feta and spinach with lemon

serves 4

200 g (7 oz) plain yoghurt
250 g (9 oz/2 cups) self-raising flour
1 tablespoon olive oil
150 g (5½ oz) minced lamb
1 garlic clove, crushed
a pinch of ground cumin
a pinch of chilli flakes
4 tablespoons tomato juice
50 g (1¾ oz) baby English spinach
100 g (3½ oz) feta cheese, crumbled
4 mint leaves, torn
olive oil, for frying
50 g (1¾ oz) butter, melted (optional)
lemon wedges, to serve

Beat the yoghurt and a pinch of salt in a large bowl until smooth. Gradually add flour until it is a stiff dough. Tip onto a lightly floured bench and gradually knead the dough, incorporating any remaining flour until it is soft and only slightly sticky. Transfer to an oiled bowl and leave, covered, for 30 minutes.

Heat the oil in a frying pan and cook the lamb until browned. Turn the heat down to medium–low and add the garlic, cumin, chilli flakes and tomato juice. Cook for another minute or until dry. Turn off the heat and leave to cook, then drain.

On a floured surface, split the dough into four equal balls. Roll each ball into a 30 cm (12 inch) circle. Place a quarter of the spinach over half of each circle, then sprinkle with a quarter of the feta, then add the lamb and mint leaves and season. Fold the dough over and seal the edges with a fork.

Preheat a barbecue flatplate or large frying pan. Brush one side of each gozleme with olive oil and cook until the base is golden. Brush the top with olive oil, turn and cook until golden.

Brush with melted butter, cut into four pieces and serve with lemon wedges.

fig, basil, buffalo mozzarella and apple balsamic salad

serves 4

8 figs

2 balls of Italian buffalo mozzarella (blue cheese or
    bocconcini can be used instead)

16 basil leaves

lemon-infused extra virgin olive oil

8 slices jamón Ibérico, prosciutto or cappacolla

apple balsamic vinegar (or aged balsamic is fine)

Tear the figs and mozzarella in half and arrange on a platter with the basil leaves. Drizzle with the olive oil and season with salt and pepper.

Tear the ham and scatter over the salad. Drizzle the apple balsamic over the top.

Hands down, this would have to be my most favourite salad to make at home. It was taught to me by a good mate and wonderful chef, John Pye, who worked alongside me for a number of years at Hugo's Bar Pizza and Hugo's Bondi. John now runs his own café in Manly, Sydney, called Café Chill. The beauty of this dish lies in its simplicity: fresh ripe figs, amazing quality buffalo mozzarella from Italy and gorgeous fresh basil leaves all lightly coated with one of the most amazing dressings I have come across. This is so good as it is, but if you want to send it off the Richter scale, try adding some paper-thin slices of Ibérico ham or some great quality prosciutto or capacolla from a trusted small goods supplier. You must try this!

If you are having a dinner party or party and want to serve something light as a canapé, try making some croûtes (thin slices of French bread, drizzled with olive oil and baked in the oven until just crisp), topped with a slice of fig, a slice of mozzarella, a basil leaf and some apple balsamic — the vegetarians will love you for it.

Churrasco is a South American way of cooking meat, usually done on a rotisserie or spit. I have an amazing barbecue at home that has a couple of rotating electric 'swords' and I'm in the habit of throwing all types of meat, seafood and vegetables onto those swords and letting them cook over the coals and sawdust until they have a lovely smoky flavour. If you don't have a super-barbie, you can just as easily roast the beef or barbecue some steaks instead.The main drawcard here is the chimichurri sauce — it's a heady mix of chillies, herbs, vinegar, oil and spices and just about dances on your taste buds.

churrasco wagyu beef with chimichurri sauce

serves 4

CHIMICHURRI SAUCE

1 large handful of flat-leaf (Italian) parsley leaves

125 ml (4 fl oz/½ cup) olive oil

4 tablespoons red wine vinegar

1 small handful of coriander (cilantro) leaves

2 garlic cloves

¾ teaspoon dried red chilli flakes

½ teaspoon ground cumin

½ teaspoon salt

1 kg (2 lb 4 oz) side of sirloin or fillet of Wagyu beef

smoked tomato salsa, opposite

To make the chimichurri sauce, blend the parsley, olive oil, vinegar, coriander, garlic, chilli, cumin and salt in a food processor. Pour over the beef, keeping about half a cupful of sauce to serve with the beef later. Marinate for 1–2 days, if you have time.

Take the beef out of the marinade and place on a rotisserie. Cook over an open flame for about 15–25 minutes, depending on how hot the flames are and how thick the meat is (you want to take the meat off the heat when it's rare and let it rest for 10 minutes before slicing).

Slice the beef and spoon the chimichurri sauce over it. Serve with some smoked tomato salsa.

smoked tomato salsa

250 g (9 oz) black turtle beans (or tinned
    kidney beans)

4 vine-ripened tomatoes, halved

4 corn cobs, roasted in the oven or blackened
    on a barbecue

150 g (5½ oz) roasted and peeled red capsicum
    (peppers), diced (or Spanish pimientos)

2 tablespoons chimichurri sauce, opposite

2 handfuls of coriander (cilantro) leaves

zest of 1 lime

2½ tablespoons lime juice

SMOKING MIXTURE

100 g (3½ oz) tea (preferably orange pekoe)

100 g (3½ oz) rice

100 g (3½ oz) brown sugar

1 cardamom pod, crushed

1 cinnamon quill, broken

a pinch of coriander seed

a pinch of peppercorns

a pinch of sichuan peppercorns

Soak the beans overnight in cold water and then drain. Place in a saucepan with three times as much water as beans. Simmer for 2 hours or until just tender, then drain and cool. (Or use tinned beans — just make sure you rinse and drain them.)

Line the base of a wok with foil and add your smoking mixture. Heat to medium–high and place a steamer tray or wire rack over the top. Place the tomatoes flesh side down on the rack and cover with the lid. Smoke for 10 minutes, then remove the lid and let the tomatoes cool before peeling them.

Chop the tomatoes into small pieces and mix with the beans, corn kernels, roasted capsicum, chimichurri sauce, coriander, lime zest and juice.

spanish jamón, marinated olives and tomato bread

spanish jamón

100 g (3½ oz) jamón Ibérico (Spanish ham)
Spanish extra virgin olive oil (if you like)

Either buy the ham already sliced from a speciality Spanish deli, top butcher or top-quality food purveyor, or (for a special occasion) buy a leg and slice it yourself. Try a slice drizzled with a little olive oil to see if you like it with or without.

marinated olives

2 cinnamon sticks
3 star anise
2 teaspoons caraway seeds
zest of 1 orange, cut into large pieces
2 teaspoons fennel seeds
2 teaspoons coriander seeds
2 teaspoons cardamom pods
½ bunch of rosemary sprigs
500 ml (17 fl oz/2 cups) extra virgin olive oil
splash of Sambucca (if you like)
500 g (1 lb 2 oz) olives

Put all the ingredients except the olives in a saucepan and heat gently for 5–10 minutes until little bubbles start to form on the top of the oil (do not boil). Add the olives and remove from the heat. Cool in the pan before serving. These can be stored in an airtight container.

Pan con tomate is Spanish for tomato bread and this is a classic recipe throughout Spain. It is delicious by itself as a starter in the summer months when tomatoes are at their best.

tomato bread

1 loaf crusty country bread, sliced

olive oil

4 garlic cloves

1 tablespoon sea salt

125 ml (4 fl oz/½ cup) extra virgin olive oil

10 very ripe tomatoes, halved

Rub the bread with a bit of olive oil and grill until crisp. Using a mortar and pestle, pound together the garlic and sea salt, then add the extra virgin olive oil.

Squeeze the tomato over the toast, squeezing out the seeds, juice and pulp. Spoon the oil, salt and garlic mixture over the bread and season with some cracked pepper.

Ibérico ham is one of the best ingredients in the world. I am in awe at how good it tastes — it would be unfair to compare it to any other ham as it has a taste all of its own. Jamón Ibérico comes from the black Iberian pigs of Spain, which are descendants of the wild boar and make up the last remaining free-grazing breed in Europe. The Ibérico pig is found exclusively in the south-western areas of the Iberian Peninsula (Spain and Portugal) and its characteristics are long, thin, strong legs, a short neck and pointed snout, dark hair and noticeably dark hooves (it is often described as 'la pata negra', the black foot). The special property of the Ibérico pig is its capacity to store fatty deposits as intra-muscular fat (marbling) in a similar fashion to the very finest Wagyu beef cattle. The pigs are fed on acorns and then expertly salted, hung and aged for about three years to produce magic. You only need a small amount, say 10–20 g per person, as it is quite rich. I think it makes a great gift —you can buy it sliced in 50 g or 100 g packs or as a whole leg to have at a wedding or party. And it's a perfect way to start a summer barbecue. Make sure you eat a bit of the fat with the meat as there is so much flavour in there (and you're paying for it anyway). You can also use the cheaper Serrano ham which tastes almost as amazing.

Most chefs have some bad eating habits; often due to working at mealtimes, rather than eating at the same time as everyone else. Often our palates can become fatigued and satiated, so we tend to eat small snack-sized meals. This has a carry-over effect into the home, so I try to make sure there are always healthy snacks on hand. I love to have good-quality olives in the house — there is nothing wrong with olives out of the jar, but if you can marinate your own with flavours you love, it's a lovely way to nibble your way through to the next meal.

oysters with campari and grapefruit granita

serves 12

2½ tablespoons Campari

1½ tablespoons Champagne, chardonnay or white
   wine vinegar

2 tablespoons sugar

100 ml (3½ fl oz) grapefruit juice

12 oysters, on crushed ice

Stir the Campari, vinegar, sugar and grapefruit juice
in a saucepan over medium heat until the sugar
dissolves. Pour into a baking tray and freeze for a
few hours. Run a fork through the frozen mixture to
rough it up into ice shavings.

Arrange your oysters on a platter of crushed ice
and serve the granita in a small bowl in the centre.

There is nothing more indulgent to eat, or easier to serve, than a platter of fresh oysters on a magnificent sunny day. The true purist will say that the only way to eat an oyster is straight from the shell with the natural juices as the dressing — no salt, no lemon, no nothing.

That is how I love to eat them myelf, but not all the time. I like to experiment with different serving suggestions, and this would have to be one of my favourites — it is very easy and yet looks so impressive.

gorgonzola, fig and pancetta pizza

serves 4

When figs are in season (which in Australia is from about November to April), I am a very happy man. They are a versatile fruit that deserve a place on every kitchen bench. Slice them over pancakes for breakfast, team them with an antipasto plate of Italian sliced meats, toss through a delicate salad, or tear them apart after dinner with some beautiful cheese... Figs truly are one of nature's great gifts.

One way I love to use figs is on a pizza (I often sneak a ball or two of pizza dough into my bag as I leave work so I can have this for dinner). I team them with creamy gorgonzola dolce latte and paper-thin slices of pancetta — what could be more addictive? If you're feeding kids and they're not huge fans of blue cheese, try this with some buffalo mozzarella or ricotta.

1 quantity pizza dough (page 153)

semolina or plain flour, for rolling pizza dough

½ quantity tomato pizza sauce (page 153)

1 handful of chopped parsley

120 g (4 oz) shredded mozzarella cheese

24 thin slices of tomato

28 slices of pancetta

180 g (6 oz) gorgonzola dolce latte, sliced

6 figs

1 handful of rocket leaves

125 ml (4 fl oz/½ cup) apple balsamic vinegar

Preheat your oven to its highest temperature. Divide the dough into four portions and roll out on a lightly floured surface until you have four thin pizza bases. Place on baking trays and prick the bases all over with a fork to stop air bubbles forming when they are cooking.

Spoon some tomato pizza sauce over each base, then sprinkle with the parsley, mozzarella, tomato, pancetta and gorgonzola. Season with salt and pepper. Bake in the oven for 5–10 minutes or until golden and crispy.

Slice the figs and arrange over the pizzas. Add some rocket leaves and drizzle with the apple balsamic vinegar.

I have a very special place for mud crabs… in my stomach. I have a good mate in the Northern Territory called Steve Travia, AKA the Fish Whisperer. We head off to his property a few hours west of Darwin and what follows is a week of hunting, fishing, drinking and laughing (not to mention hard work). We put our pots out on the first day (usually very early, depending on the tides) and at sunset, on our way home from a 10-hour fishing session, we check the traps and generally have enough for a feed. So, mud crab is on the menu nightly, alongside barramundi, coral trout, golden snapper, mojitos, beers — you get the picture. Anyway as mud crabs grow like weeds up there we've created many delicious recipes to get rid of the darned things… it's a bloody tough life being an Aussie (or a mud crab).

chilli mud crab

serves 4

4 live mud crabs

125 ml (4 fl oz/½ cup) oil

8 garlic cloves, chopped

4 banana chillies, chopped

4 tablespoons julienned fresh ginger

2 tablespoons chopped coriander (cilantro) root

250 ml (9 fl oz/1 cup) tomato sauce (ketchup)

125 ml (4 fl oz/½ cup) sweet chilli sauce

375 ml (13 fl oz/1½ cups) chicken stock

125 ml (4 fl oz/½ cup) hoisin sauce

2 tablespoons fish sauce

1–2 tablespoons sugar

2 teaspoons sea salt

1 handful of chopped spring onion (scallions),
    green part only

1 handful of mixed mint, Vietnamese mint and
    coriander (cilantro) leaves

1 punnet of cherry tomatoes, cut in half

Put the mud crabs in the freezer for about an hour or two until they are unconscious. Remove the top shell by lifting the flap on the underside. Remove the gills (the spongy grey fingers) and any muck by rinsing very lightly and quickly under running water.

Using a cleaver, cut the crabs in half lengthways, then cut into three on each side. Crack the claws with the back of a knife or cleaver so they open a bit to let the sauce in.

Heat the oil in a large wok and cook the garlic, chilli, ginger and coriander root until fragrant. Add the crabs and toss for a minute until they change colour. Add the tomato sauce, chilli sauce, stock (or water), hoisin sauce, fish sauce, sugar and salt, stir well and bring to the boil. Cover and simmer for about 10 minutes. Add the spring onions, herbs and cherry tomatoes. Serve with steamed jasmine rice, crab crackers, crab pickers, finger bowls and bibs.

pipis in foil on the barbecue

serves 4

This is a no-fuss, no-nonsense way to cook something a little bit different for your guests. A starter on the barbie is sure to impress — the great thing about this is that it's easy and you can use any seafood you want: pieces of flathead, prawns, squid or mussels. The ocean's the limit, as they say (or don't say). You need foil, butter, garlic, chilli, herbs, lemon and the freshest seafood possible — in this case we're using pipis because I think they're underrated, cheap and thoroughly sensational, so I want to give them a bit of good publicity. If you like, you can cook some pasta and toss it through at the end. And, if you want to show off, grate some bottarga over the top.

1 kg (2 lb 4 oz) pipis

3 tablespoons butter

2 tablespoons extra virgin olive oil

2 tablespoons chopped garlic

1 tablespoon chopped long red chilli

2 tablespoons chopped parsley

2 tablespoons white wine

zest and juice of 1 lemon

1 teaspoon grated bottarga (if you like)

Line two large bowls with a double layer of foil. Mix together the pipis, butter, olive oil, garlic, chilli, parsley, wine, lemon zest and juice then divide between the two bowls. Seal the foil at the top to make two packages.

Place the packages on a preheated barbecue or in a 180°C (350°F/Gas 4) oven and cook for about 5 minutes or until the pipis open up and are cooked. Give them a good shake to make sure they are coated in the mixture.

Sprinkle with the grated bottarga to serve. I like to mop up the juices with some fresh bread.

NOTE Bottarga is the dried pressed roe of the mullet or tuna and is available at speciality food stores. Alternatively, add 1 chopped anchovy at the beginning.

polenta-crusted spatchcock with green olive salsa

serves 4

I like to cook spatchcock at home for something different — I enjoy eating meat on the bone and with spatchcock I can get the delicious flavour but in a much shorter time than if I were using a normal-sized chicken. This dish uses a mixture of polenta and breadcrumbs to crumb the bird, which gives it a bit more texture — I want to team it with a dressed salad of sorts, so the crumb needs to have some crunch. The 'salad' is a delicious salsa of green olives, parsley, celery and lemon that works well with seafood too. This is a dish that everyone will love, including the kids; although you might just serve it with some lemon wedges if they aren't too keen on olives.

ONION CONFIT

150 g (5½ oz/1 cup) chopped onion

250 ml (9 fl oz/1 cup) olive oil

200 ml (7 fl oz) veal stock

100 g (3½ oz/⅔ cup) coarse polenta

60 g (2 oz/⅔ cup) grated parmesan cheese

4 tablespoons chopped parsley

4 x 500 g (1 lb 2 oz) spatchcocks (poussins),
   butterflied and cut into quarters

grapeseed oil, for frying

115 g (4 oz/⅔ cup) pitted green olives

2 tablespoons diced celery

2 tablespoons chopped parsley

2 tablespoons lemon juice

125 ml (4 fl oz/½ cup) extra virgin olive oil

To make the onion confit, put the onion and olive oil in a saucepan over low heat and cook for 2 hours or until soft. You need 2 tablespoons for this recipe — keep any leftover in a screw-top jar in the fridge.

Heat the veal stock in a saucepan over medium heat until reduced by half. Preheat the oven to 180°C (350°F/Gas 4).

Mix together the polenta, parmesan, parsley and some sea salt and pepper. Rub the spatchcocks with olive oil, then coat well with the crumb mixture.

Heat the grapeseed oil and shallow-fry the spatchcocks until golden on both sides. Transfer to a roasting tin and cook in the oven for 5 minutes, or until cooked through so that the juices run clear.

Mix the green olives, celery, onion confit, parsley, lemon juice and extra virgin olive oil together and season with salt and pepper. Spoon green olive salsa onto a plate, add a spatchcock and then more salsa. Finish with a spoonful of veal jus.

tomato, buffalo mozzarella and olive salad

serves 4

4 vine-ripened tomatoes, cut into wedges
1 French shallot, finely sliced
2 balls of Italian buffalo mozzarella
16 basil leaves
3 tablespoons extra virgin olive oil
1 tablespoon aged balsamic vinegar
20 olives (Ligurian or manzanillo)
grissini (Italian bread sticks), to serve (if you like)

Arrange the tomatoes on a platter with the sliced shallot. Tear the mozzarella and scatter over the top with the basil leaves.

Drizzle the olive oil and balsamic over the salad, scatter with olives and season with salt and pepper. Serve with grissini.

risotto of whiting, peas and bottarga

serves 4

This dish really goes to show how few ingredients you need to make a beautiful meal. Last summer I was fishing with my brother-in-law, Udo, and we caught quite a few whiting off the rocks at Bondi in a very short period of time. It was just one of those rare afternoons when everything worked in our favour: not too many swimmers, a great sunset, lots of hungry fish. I took a few fillets home, not knowing what to do with them, and after going through the fridge I found only some fresh peas (yes, my fridge isn't always jam-packed with culinary delicacies) and some bottarga in the freezer. We have a small herb garden with fresh mint growing, so I thought why not try whipping up a risotto with these ingredients? I was a bit nervous (I didn't want those poor whiting to have died for a sub-standard meal), but the end result was one of the finer dishes I have ever cooked at home. I will definitely make this again when the whiting are biting.

500 ml (17 fl oz/2 cups) chicken stock

160 g (5½ oz/1 cup) fresh shelled peas (or frozen)

4 garlic cloves, finely chopped

1 onion, finely sliced

2 tablespoons butter

2 tablespoons olive oil

200 g (7 oz) arborio rice

250 ml (9 fl oz/1 cup) white wine (I used pinot grigio)

1 handful of mint leaves

a pinch of chilli flakes

300 g (10½ oz) whiting fillets with skin, cut into large pieces

2 tablespoons lemon-infused olive oil

1 tablespoon grated bottarga (dried mullet roe)

lime wedges, to serve (if you like)

Put the chicken stock in a large saucepan and bring to the boil, then add the peas and cook for 3 minutes.

Fry the garlic and onion with the butter and oil in a large saucepan over medium heat until soft. Add the rice and cook for another minute, stirring with a wooden spoon so the rice is well coated. Increase the heat and add the wine, then stir for about 1 minute until the wine has disappeared. Pour in the stock through a sieve (keeping the peas in the sieve), stir and reduce the heat to medium–low. Cook for about 12 minutes, stirring often.

When the rice is nearly cooked, add the mint, chilli, whiting and peas and season with salt and pepper. Cook for a further minute, stirring, until the rice is cooked and the fish just cooked through.

Spoon onto serving plates and drizzle with the lemon-infused olive oil and grated bottarga. Serve with lime wedges if you like.

sashimi with japanese soy dressing

serves 4

200 g (7 oz) sashimi-grade fish (tuna, ocean trout,
    atlantic salmon, kingfish, scallops or prawns)
wasabi, to taste
pickled ginger (if you like)

JAPANESE SOY DRESSING
2 tablespoons sake
3 tablespoons mirin
250 ml (9 fl oz/1 cup) dark soy sauce
3 tablespoons tamari (Japanese soy sauce)
10 g (¼ oz) dried bonito flakes
1 teaspoon grapeseed oil

To make the dressing, combine the sake and mirin in a saucepan over medium heat and burn off the alcohol. Add the dark soy sauce, tamari, dried bonito flakes and grapeseed oil, then transfer to a bowl and leave overnight in a cool, dark place.

Strain the liquid through muslin or cheesecloth and store in a cool, dark place.

Slice your fish with a very sharp knife and arrange on a platter with wasabi and pickled ginger. Serve with the dressing.

A lot of the country's finest restaurant menus have one thing in common at the moment — raw fish. Whether it is a tartare, carpaccio or slices of sashimi, I am always drawn to raw fish as a starter choice. I know it won't fill me up, so I can still enjoy the next course, and ultimately a dessert or cheese plate at the end of the meal.

To serve raw fish at home is a lot easier than you might think: the only prerequisite is a sharp knife and the best quality seafood you can get your hands on. When you visit the fish markets or your fishmonger, you'll see a section called 'sashimi-grade'. These are the best pieces of fish available that the fishmonger has trimmed into a skinless boneless fillet, perfect for slicing up into sashimi, dicing into tartare or rolling out into carpaccio. The most commonly available sashimi-grade fish are yellow- and blue-fin tuna, ocean trout, Atlantic or New Zealand king salmon and hiramasa kingfish (a farmed, increased-fat kingfish from South Australia). Other varieties I like to try are snapper, paper thin-sliced whiting, scallops, lobster and cuttlefish. So next time you're at the fish markets, give raw fish a go — team it with this dressing, and you could be eating at one of the country's finest restaurants in your own home.

caramelised endive tarts with seared scallops

makes 24

4 heads of endive (witlof)
2 tablespoons butter
3 tablespoons soft brown sugar
3 tablespoons orange juice
2 sheets frozen puff pastry, thawed
1 free-range egg, lightly beaten
24 scallops
2 tablespoons salmon caviar

Chop the endive into 2.5 cm (1 inch) thick pieces. Fry in the butter in a large frying pan until it softens a bit, then add some sugar to sweeten. Cook until caramelised, then add the orange juice and cook until all the liquid has evaporated. Season with salt and pepper, then remove from the heat and leave to cool. Preheat the oven to 200°C (400°F/Gas 6). Lightly grease a tin of 24 small tart or muffin holes.

Spoon endive into the bottom of each tart hole. Top with a circle of puff pastry the same size as the hole. Brush with egg and bake until golden.

Sear some scallops until golden in a touch of oil in a frying pan over medium–high heat. Flip over for 10 seconds and remove from the heat.

Turn out the endive tarts onto a platter. Top each one with a seared scallop and a little salmon caviar.

These are really nice canapés to serve at a party: small, elegant and super tasty, which is exactly what you're after with bite-size portions. I really love the flavour combination in this dish: caramelised bitter endive simmered with orange juice and sugar, teamed with crisp puff pastry and scallops. Without doubt, scallops would have to be one of the finest ingredients to come from the ocean. These could also be served as a starter with a larger pastry case and four scallops instead, and with a watercress salad on top.

porcetto arrosto — giovanni's oven-roasted suckling pig

serves 4

Quite a few recipes I make at home have ended up on my table through eating at friends' restaurants. Since I have had the kids, my days of eating out have decreased drastically. The plus side of that is now I get to spend more time at home doing what I love — cooking.

I do still make time to visit one my of favourite restaurants… this recipe was given to me by Giovanni Pilu from Pilu in Sydney's Freshwater. He is Sardinian and his restaurant is one of my all-time favourite places to eat in Australia. It overlooks one of the country's best beaches and he has some of the friendliest staff in town. This is one of his signature dishes.

½ **suckling pig, halved lengthways (about 2.5 kg/**
    5 lb 8 oz), head removed
40 g (1½ oz) sea salt
olive oil
rosemary sprigs

APPLE SAUCE
50 g (1¾ oz) butter
6 granny smith apples, peeled, cored and sliced
3 tablespoons sugar
a pinch of ground cinnamon
3 cloves, ground
1½ tablespoons vermouth

Place the suckling pig, skin side up, in a large oiled roasting tin. Cover the skin generously with sea salt and rub in thoroughly, then leave for 15 minutes or until the skin becomes moist. Drizzle oil liberally over the skin and rub in well, then sprinkle with extra sea salt. Preheat the oven to 150°C (300°F/Gas 2).

Roast the pig on the lowest shelf of the oven for 2 hours or until the skin starts to come away from the top of the meat. Remove from the oven and brush the salt off the skin. Increase the oven to 220°C (425°F/Gas 7). Return the pig to the oven for about 10 minutes or until the skin becomes crisp.

Transfer the pig on a chopping board, cover with foil and leave for 10 minutes, then cut into pieces.

To make the apple sauce, melt the butter in a large frying pan over low heat. Add the apples and cook for about 10 minutes. Add the sugar, cinnamon, cloves and vermouth. Cover and cook, stirring occasionally, until the apples are soft but still chunky.

Serve large chunks of pork with sprigs of rosemary and the apple sauce.

NOTE You can order suckling pig from speciality butchers.

harissa lamb leg with roasted pumpkin, feta and pomegranate salad

serves 4

Mmm, roast lamb… how good is it when you're going to someone's house for dinner and they tell you they're cooking roast lamb? Or, even better, when you come home from work, open the front door and smell lamb roasting in your own home? This is how I cook it when I want to spice things up a bit. Harissa is a North African spice paste made of chillies, garlic, cumin, coriander and olive oil and is very seductive when used sparingly — it excites the palate and leaves you craving more. Here I have teamed the lamb with a very simple roast pumpkin salad and used a beautiful dressing made from pomegranate molasses, a jar of which deserves a place in every pantry.

1 lamb leg (2–3 kg/4 lb 8 oz–6 lb 12 oz), bone in

4 tablespoons harissa paste

1 tablespoon extra virgin olive oil

Bring the lamb leg to room temperature (and make sure you know how much it weighs). Preheat the oven to 180°C (350°F/Gas 4). Coat the lamb with the harissa paste, then with the olive oil.

Roast the lamb for 45 minutes, and then another 25 minutes per kilo of weight. Remove from the oven and leave to rest, loosely covered with foil, for about 30 minutes. Slice and serve with the salad.

roasted pumpkin, feta and pomegranate salad

600 g (1 lb 5 oz) pumpkin, unpeeled and chopped

1 small red onion, cut into wedges

a pinch of ground cumin

a pinch of chilli flakes

1 tablespoon extra virgin olive oil

1 handful of mint leaves

120 g (4 oz) sheep's milk feta (Persian is great)

2 tablespoons pine nuts, roasted

1–2 tablespoons pomegranate molasses

2 tablespoons pomegranate seeds

Preheat the oven to 200°C (400°F/Gas 6). Put the pumpkin and onion in a roasting tin and toss with the cumin, chilli flakes and some sea salt and pepper. Drizzle with the olive oil and roast until golden. Toss with the mint, feta and pine nuts. Drizzle with the pomegranate molasses and pomegranate seeds before serving.

salt and pepper bugs with shaoxing

serves 4

2 teaspoons salt

2 teaspoons white peppercorns

1 teaspoon black peppercorns

1 teaspoon sichuan peppercorns

2 tablespoons vegetable oil

3 cm (1¼ inch) piece ginger, finely grated

3 garlic cloves, finely chopped

12 Moreton Bay or Balmain bugs, halved, coral
    removed from heads, deveined

3 tablespoons shoaxing rice wine (or dry sherry)

2 teaspoons sugar

4 spring onions (scallions), thinly sliced

1 small handful of coriander (cilantro) leaves

lemon wedges, to serve

Combine the salt and the peppercorns in a mortar and pound with the pestle until finely crushed.

Heat the oil in a wok and add the ginger, garlic and half of the salt and pepper mixture. Stir-fry for 1–2 minutes or until very fragrant. Add the bugs and stir-fry until almost cooked. Combine the shaoxing rice wine and sugar and add to the wok. Bring to the boil, cover and simmer for 5 minutes.

Toss in the spring onions and half the coriander.

Serve immediately with the remaining coriander, salt and pepper mixture and the lemon wedges.

The new fast food is seafood. If only everyone in the western world would or could embrace that fact, imagine the great health and vitality that would come from such a diet. We could completely replace the prepackaged processed stodge that so many people see these days as fast food. As my brother-in-law, Udo, says whenever anyone asks his political or religious views: 'A fresh fish makes a damned fine meal, mate'. I couldn't agree more, and this is a great way to add some spice to a fresh piece of fish or crustacean.

robbo's ribs

serves 4

I have a good mate called Robbo (Michael Roberts) and we often go out on the harbour together fishing, or have a get-together for Boxing Day or New Year's Eve. Michael is famous for, among other things, his ribs. He has spent quite a bit of time living in the States, hence his love of barbecued ribs. When I go out on the boat with him, I will sometimes bring along some prawns and oysters and other chef-type delicacies, and Robbo will always show up with his ribs. And, do you know something, everyone always goes for Robbo's ribs over anything else on offer. Robbo, you are a legend — thanks for sharing your 'secret' recipe with everyone.

3 racks pork spare ribs
240 g (8½ oz) jar lee kum kee rib sauce

Cut the ribs into single pieces. Put in a large bowl with the sauce and marinate for about 20 minutes.

Preheat a barbecue to medium–high. Cook the ribs for 12–20 minutes, depending on their thickness (turning over when necessary) — they should be a little bit blackened for extra flavour.

prawn rolls

serves 4

This is another fantastically simple meal to take on your next picnic. Buy good-quality bread rolls, make up the prawn mix and keep it separate, chilled in the esky, until you arrive at your lunch spot so the rolls don't go soggy. Endeavour prawns from north Queensland are the sweetest and best for this recipe but you could easily use any other cooked prawns, crab meat or even roast chicken.

350 g (12 oz) cooked and peeled prawns
80 g (2½ oz) thinly sliced celery
160 g (5¾ oz/⅔ cup) mayonnaise
4 tablespoons spiced tomato or chilli relish (or sweet chilli)
1 handful of tarragon leaves (or other herbs such as parsley, basil or chives)
juice of ½ lemon
4 bread rolls
1 large handful of shredded iceberg lettuce

Stir together the prawns, celery, mayonnaise, tomato sauce, herbs and lemon juice and season with salt and pepper.

Slice the bread rolls in half without cutting all the way through, and butter them if you like. When you're ready to eat, fill the rolls with the prawn mixture and a little shredded lettuce.

vongole with fregola

serves 4

The Sardinians of Italy have a wonderful relationship with the ocean and it shows with dishes such as this. The use of fregola really lifts this dish from one dimension into something beautiful that is just made for sharing with friends and family. Fregola is Sardinia's very hard pasta, the size of match heads, that expands when cooked to look rather like large couscous and takes on the flavour of the sauce. Serve this with some crusty bread and a green leaf salad for a great lunch.

125 ml (4 fl oz/½ cup) extra virgin olive oil

3 garlic cloves, finely chopped

2 tablespoons chopped onion

1 long red chilli, finely chopped

800 g (1 lb 12 oz) vongole (Italian clams)

40 g (1½ oz) fregola

625 g (1 lb 6 oz/2½ cups) tinned tomatoes, crushed

12 basil leaves, torn

310 ml (11 fl oz/1¼ cups) fish stock or water

zest of ½ lemon

1–2 tablespoons butter

Gently heat the oil, garlic, onion and chilli in a large saucepan until starting to colour. Stir in the vongole and then the fregola.

Add the tomatoes, basil and fish stock and cook over low heat until the vongole open and the fregola is tender. Season to taste with sea salt and cracked pepper and add the lemon zest. Add the butter and leave to rest for 5 minutes before serving.

barbecued seared scallops with sauce vierge

serves 4

20 scallops on the half shell

1 tablespoon extra virgin olive oil

2 tablespoons chervil leaves, to garnish

SAUCE VIERGE

4 tablespoons extra virgin olive oil

1 tablespoon lemon juice

1 teaspoon roasted coriander seeds, crushed

½ teaspoon roasted fennel seeds, crushed

8 basil leaves, very finely sliced

2 tablespoons finely diced fennel

2 ripe tomatoes, peeled, deseeded and diced

Make sure your scallops are close to room temperature before cooking (they shouldn't be cold as we are eating them rare). Remove the scallops from their shells and set aside.

To make the sauce vierge, gently warm the oil in a saucepan. Remove from the heat and mix in the lemon juice, coriander and fennel seeds, and leave for a minute. Add the basil, fennel and tomato and season with salt and pepper. Set aside and preheat your barbecue to hot, if using.

Toss the scallops in the oil and season lightly with sea salt and white pepper. Cook the scallops on the barbecue, or in a frying pan over high heat, for about 30 seconds on each side so they are cooked rare.

Put the scallops back on their shells and dress with the sauce vierge and chervil.

This is a classic recipe that appeared in one of the first cookbooks I ever bought: *Wild Food from Land and Sea*, by the legendary chef Marco Pierre White. At the time of publication he was considered one of the finest and most 'colourful' chefs in the world, and I loved the way the food looked in his books and the techniques he used to create the dishes. This is a slight variation on his recipe as I have added fresh fennel and fennel seeds to the dressing to add a little extra crunch. I love the aniseed flavour the fennel brings to the scallops.

snapper 'aqua pazza' or fish in crazy water

serves 4

I was filming my TV series FISH up in Cairns and having a magic day… we'd caught huge trevally, a near-record Spanish mackerel, magnificent red emperor and coral trout, but the highlight for me was a fish I'd never even heard of before… Locally it's known as a frying-pan snapper (it looks like a snapper but with elongated spines on its dorsal fin) and in my excitement I cooked this classic Italian recipe.

4 frying-pan snappers (or other firm white fish)

8 garlic cloves, roasted and peeled

1 long red chilli, roasted, peeled and sliced

1 punnet of cherry tomatoes

20 ligurian olives (or marinated small olives)

1.5 litres (52 fl oz/6 cups) sparkling mineral water

3 tablespoons butter

1 large handful of basil leaves

lemon wedges, to serve

Make three cuts down to the bone on each side of the fish. Heat a little oil in a frying pan and cook the fish for 3–4 minutes until golden (cook each one separately, using a quarter of the ingredients, and keeping them warm as you go). Turn the fish and add the garlic, chilli, tomato, olives and some salt and pepper. After 30 seconds, add the mineral water (just enough to cover the fish), butter and basil and cook for another couple of minutes until the fish is just done. Serve with lemon wedges and the sauce.

I had the most amazing childhood growing up on Queensland's sunny Gold Coast. My days consisted of waking up at 5:30 am, riding my bicycle down to the beach with my surfboard under my arm, surfing for two hours, going to school and then doing it all over again in the afternoon. Until the weekend, when I rode my bike down to the beach in the morning and came home after dark (where did that hard life go?) The thing I loved most about the weekends, apart from the surf and the freedom, were the steak sandwiches from the local milk bar. I still serve my version of the timeless steak sandwich regularly at my barbecues… but do remember this is best eaten with your feet in the sand, watching the waves.

steak sandwich with sweet and sour onions, rocket and aïoli

serves 4

SWEET AND SOUR ONIONS

2 tablespoons olive oil

1 large onion, thinly sliced

2 tablespoons sugar

2 tablespoons balsamic vinegar

4 x 85 g (3 oz) medallions of eye fillet steak

1 teaspoon finely chopped rosemary

8 slices of ciabatta (or bread of your choice)

4 tablespoons extra virgin olive oil

2 tablespoons aïoli (page 40) or mayonnaise

1 handful of rocket

2 tablespoons of your favourite tomato chutney

To make the sweet and sour onions, heat the oil in a pan and cook the onion, stirring, until just starting to colour. Add the sugar and balsamic and simmer until it has almost a jam consistency. Season with salt.

Preheat the barbecue, if you are using. Lightly bash the steaks with a meat tenderiser. Season the steak with salt and pepper and add the rosemary and a touch of olive oil. Barbecue or cook in a frying pan for 1–2 minutes until seared and sealed on one side. Turn over and cook for half the time you cooked the first side, then remove from the heat and leave to rest for 1–2 minutes to let the juices settle.

Brush each slice of bread lightly with olive oil and place onto the barbecue grill for about 30 seconds until marks start to appear. Don't turn the bread over (we are only toasting the outside so the inside of the sandwich stays nice and soft).

Spread four slices of the toast, on their soft side, with aïoli. Top with the rocket, tomato chutney, steak and onions. Put the tops on the sandwiches, wrap in baking paper and cut in half. Serve with an icy cold Aussie beer.

seared yellow-fin tuna with fennel, lemon, olives and parsley

serves 4

One of my first regular customers at Hugo's 13 years ago was Deborah Hutton. Since then we have gone on to be good friends and one of the joys I have in my job, hosting *Fresh* on Channel 9, is that my friends drop by the studio and cook some recipes with me. Deb was in last year and did a segment called 'stolen recipes' — this is her amazing dish with tuna, lemon, olives and fennel. The thing to remember here is that the salad is part of the dish, so it's up to you how you serve it: on top, underneath or on the side. The salad also works well with any whole cooked fish, but I prefer the oilier species like tuna, salmon, kingfish and Spanish mackerel.

4 x 180 g (6 oz) sashimi-grade yellow-fin or blue-fin tuna steaks

2 large fennel bulbs

4 lemons, peeled and cut into segments

125 g (4½ oz/1 cup) pitted olives of your choice

1 large handful of flat-leaf (Italian) parsley

1 bird's eye chilli, finely chopped

4 tablespoons lemon-infused extra virgin olive oil

2 tablespoons olive oil

Preheat your barbecue to very hot, if using. Let the tuna steaks reach room temperature before cooking.

Slice the white part of the fennel bulb as thinly as possible. Toss together the fennel, lemon, olives, parsley, chilli, lemon-infused olive oil and some salt and pepper.

Brush the tuna with oil and cook on your barbecue or in a frying pan for about 1 minute on each side, (the outside should be seared and the inside rare). Serve with the salad.

sugarcane prawn skewers (chao tom)

serves 4

I first ate this in Vietnam and, like the food of so many countries, it varies a little from place to place, depending on which produce is in season at the time. My favourite accompaniments are the fresh Asian herbs (a must: Vietnamese mint, fresh mint, Thai basil, coriander) and some fresh vegies like lettuce, carrot, bean sprouts and cucumber. It's all tied together with the most delicious and easy dipping sauce known. You don't need to use the skewers if you don't want to; just make patties and cook.

1 kg (2 lb 4 oz) raw king prawns, peeled,
    deveined and diced
1 tablespoon fish sauce
1 teaspoon sugar
1 garlic clove, finely chopped
1 hot red chilli, finely chopped
1 spring onion (scallion), finely sliced
2 tablespoons ice-cold water
4 sugarcane sticks (bought in tins at Asian
    supermarkets)
4 tablespoons vegetable oil
1 butter lettuce
1 Lebanese cucumber, seeds removed and sliced
1 carrot, peeled and cut into strips
about 150 g (5 oz/1–2 cups) bean sprouts, trimmed
a selection of fresh herbs, such as Vietnamese mint,
    Thai basil and coriander (cilantro) leaves
Vietnamese dipping sauce (opposite, or hoisin
    sauce)
lime dipping sauce (opposite)

Process the prawns in a food processor until smooth and sticky. Add the fish sauce, sugar, garlic, chilli and spring onion and pulse to just combine, then add the cold water. Cut the sugar cane into 1 cm (½ inch) thick sticks.

Preheat a barbecue plate or chargrill. Brush your hands with oil and divide the prawn mixture into eight equal portions. Wrap the mixture around the middle of each sugar cane stick, leaving the ends free. Brush the sticks and the barbecue with oil and cook them for 5 minutes, turning occasionally, until golden and cooked through.

Arrange the vegetables, herbs and prawn skewers on a platter with bowls of the dipping sauces, letting guests help themselves. To eat, peel the chao tom from the sugarcane sticks, wrap in lettuce leaves with the vegetables and herbs, and dip in the sauce.

vietnamese dipping sauce

125 ml (4 fl oz/½ cup) hoisin sauce

3 tablespoons coconut cream

2 tablespoons chopped red Asian shallot

3 tablespoons rice vinegar

2 tablespoons chopped roasted peanuts

Put the hoisin sauce, coconut cream and shallot in a small pan with 125 ml (4 fl oz/½ cup) of water and simmer for 8 minutes over medium heat until thick enough to coat the back of a spoon. Leave to cool, then place in a serving bowl and top with the roasted peanuts.

lime dipping sauce

1 small red chilli, roughly chopped

1 garlic clove, chopped

1 teaspoon sugar

2 tablespoons fish sauce

juice of 2 limes

Pound the chilli and garlic with a mortar and pestle until smooth. Stir in the remaining ingredients and 3 tablespoons water. Taste and adjust the flavours if necessary.

The 'wow factor' is the best thing about cooking for friends and family and even yourself (actually, I always put myself at the top of the list when I'm deciding what to cook... selfish, I know, but if I'm cooking I want the best). And I don't mean dishes that require a degree to construct, or an internship at a 3-Michelin-star restaurant to put together; the wow factor is simply how good the food tastes and how easy it is to make that happen. That is what I strive for in my home cooking: simplicity with great flavour. This dish does all that and more — it really lets the fish speak for itself with just an added chorus from some great supporting ingredients. You can use any whole fish for this (just remember to cook it for 15 minutes per kilo), but I love the flavour of ocean trout or Atlantic salmon. It just melts in your mouth and those omega 3s are an added bonus.

whole roasted ocean trout with lemon and herbs

serves 4

3 kg (6 lb 12 oz) whole ocean trout
1 small bunch of thyme
1 small bunch of oregano
1 lemon, halved and thickly sliced
8 garlic cloves, halved
1½ tablespoons olive oil

Preheat the oven to 190°C (375°F/Gas 5). Line a large baking tray with baking paper and scatter one third of the thyme, oregano, lemon and garlic across it diagonally.

Place the fish on top of the herbs and lemon and fill its cavity with the remaining herbs, lemon and garlic. Season well with salt and pepper. Drizzle the fish with the olive oil and roast for 45 minutes.

Check the fish is cooked by inserting a metal skewer into the thickest part of it. Hold the skewer there for 10 seconds and when you pull it out check that the skewer is hot by touching it on the inside of your wrist. If the skewer is hot, then the fish is cooked. If it is only warm, the fish should be cooked for another 10–15 minutes before re-checking.

Serve the fish with the potato, egg and watercress salad (opposite) or flake the trout through the salad.

potato, egg and watercress salad with apple cider vinegar

serves 4

2 small potatoes, peeled and chopped into
    2 cm (¾ inch) cubes
1 tablespoon apple cider vinegar
3 tablespoons extra virgin olive oil
1 garlic clove, crushed
1 teaspoon sugar
leaves from 1 bunch of watercress
2 hard-boiled free-range eggs, peeled
    and crumbled

Place the potatoes in a saucepan of cold salted water and bring to a simmer. Cook until tender, then drain.

Mix together the apple cider vinegar, olive oil, garlic, sugar, 1 tablespoon of water and some salt and pepper.

Lightly toss together the watercress, potato and egg in a large bowl and dress with the apple cider vinegar dressing.

yabbie linguine

serves 4

One place in Australia that is very special to me is far north Queensland. My partner, Astrid, lived there for some time and we have a few very close friends up that way. We always make time to stop into the Salsa Bar, which is Port Douglas's premier restaurant. It has a wonderful atmosphere and the food is always exciting — they tend to embrace the amazing produce that far north Queensland is famed for and turn it into something extraordinary. But, like every good restaurant, they have a signature dish that never changes (and it had better not, either)... Theirs is their yabbie linguine and it would have to be one of my favourite things to eat in the world. I cook it at home quite regularly, substituting prawns, crab, mushrooms or even cherry tomatoes for the yabbies. I would like to thank Bill (the chef and owner of the Salsa Bar) for his recipe. If you are ever up that way pop in and say g'day; you won't be disappointed.

12 large yabbies

8 garlic cloves, crushed

2 long red chillies

125 ml (4 fl oz/½ cup) extra virgin olive oil

400 g (14 oz) fresh linguine

3 tablespoons chopped parsley

100 g (3½ oz) shaved parmesan

Put the yabbies in the freezer for 45 minutes or until they're inactive. Take out and cut in half lengthways, then clean out any muck and remove the intestinal tract.

Cook the garlic and chilli with the olive oil in a frying pan over low heat until softened but not coloured. Add the yabbies and cook on both sides until changed in colour and cooked through. You might need to cook the yabbies in two batches or use two pans, so you don't overcrowd the pan.

Cook the pasta in a saucepan of boiling salted water for 2–3 minutes until just tender, stirring occasionally with a fork to prevent the linguine from sticking.

Strain the pasta and toss through with yabbies and parsley and season to taste. Top with shaved parmesan and serve immediately.

blood orange sorbet with champagne

serves 4

1 litre (35 fl oz/4 cups) freshly squeezed
    blood orange juice (or ordinary orange juice),
    strained (about 9 large oranges)
mint leaves
500 ml (17 fl oz/2 cups) champagne

STOCK SYRUP
630 g (1 lb 6 oz) caster (superfine) sugar
1 cinnamon stick
2 star anise
zest of 1 orange

To make the stock syrup, place all the ingredients in a saucepan with 525 ml (18 fl oz) of water and bring to the boil. Remove from the heat and leave to cool, then strain.

Mix together the stock syrup and orange juice. Churn in an ice-cream machine for 20–30 minutes following the manufacturer's instructions, and then put in the freezer to firm.

Serve scoops of the sorbet with mint leaves and a a good splash of champagne. Serve immediately.

Simple and refreshing should be the call for a summer dessert, and what could fit the brief better than this one? It's a bit of a staple at my house — I always have a bottle of champagne in the fridge (for some reason I seem to receive champagne as a gift more often than anything else... obviously I'm not complaining). As far as the gelato or sorbet goes, you can make your own if you have a machine or just go down to the local gelateria or supermarket and buy some. I find the flavours that work best for this are white peach, blood orange, raspberry, strawberry and even lemon.

chocolate and hazelnut pizza with banana

serves 6

Dessert pizzas are something you must try at least once to know how good they are. This is one I have been making at Hugo's Bar Pizza and The Pantry for years and there are no strict rules to eating it. It's best to use a good-quality chocolate-hazelnut spread from Italy, but whatever's in your cupboard will probably be fine. Alternatively, use chocolate truffles or chocolate buttons on top of the dough, then you need some ripe bananas and a good-quality ice cream or gelato of your choice (I love the traditional vanilla but chocolate, banana or hazelnut would all be great). You could even use just thick cream or sweet mascarpone.

1 quantity of pizza dough (page 153)

12 tablespoons chocolate-hazelnut spread or
  32 chocolate truffles

3 bananas, sliced and coated in lemon juice

6 scoops of vanilla ice cream or gelato

6 tablespoons chocolate shavings

3 tablespoons roasted and peeled
  hazelnuts, chopped

icing (confectioners') sugar, to dust

Preheat your oven to its highest temperature. Divide the dough into six portions and roll out on a lightly floured surface until you have four thin pizza bases. Place on baking trays and prick the bases all over with a fork to stop air bubbles forming when they are cooking.

Spread the bases with the chocolate-hazelnut spread. Top with the banana slices.

Bake in the oven for 5–10 minutes or until crispy (do not burn the chocolate).

To serve, top with ice cream, chocolate shavings and chopped hazelnuts and sprinkle with icing sugar.

goat's curd cheesecake with passionfruit sauce

serves 8–10

This is one recipe that is super easy to make and always stands out as the crowd favourite. You can team it with just about any fruit in season… and I know goat's curd doesn't sound like a great cheese to put into a dessert but, trust me, this is an absolute winner.

BASE

140 g (5 oz) almonds, roasted and cooled

2 teaspoons white sesame seeds

70 g (2½ oz) butter

canola oil spray

400 ml (14 fl oz) cream

300 g (10½ oz) goat's curd

150 g (5½ oz) caster (superfine) sugar

zest and juice of 1 lemon

3 gelatine leaves or 3 teaspoons powdered gelatine

PASSIONFRUIT SAUCE

250 g (9 oz) passionfruit pulp

125 g (4½ oz) sugar

To make the base, blend the almonds and sesame seeds in a food processor. Melt the butter in a frying pan until it turns brown, then pour just enough into the nut mixture to combine.

Spray a 20 cm (8 inch) springform cake tin with canola oil. Line the base and side with baking paper, then spray with oil. Press the base mixture into the tin and leave to set in the fridge.

Gently heat the cream, goat's curd, sugar and lemon in a pan. Soak the gelatine leaves in 250 ml (9 fl oz/1 cup) cold water for 2 minutes, then squeeze out the water. Whisk into the pan of cream, then strain it all into a bowl. If using powdered gelatine, stir it into 3 tablespoons of boiling water, leave to sit for 1 minute, then add to the cream.

Pour the cream filling into the tin and leave to set for 4–5 hours in the fridge.

To make the passionfruit sauce, blend the pulp, then strain to separate the juice. Measure the juice and then add an equal amount of water. Put the sugar in a saucepan with 1 cm (½ inch) of water over medium–high heat and boil until caramel. Add the juice and water mixture and cook until syrupy, then add the passionfruit seeds. Leave to cool slightly. Cut the cheesecake with a hot knife and serve with the sauce.

sago pudding with roasted spiced pineapple

serves 4

My kids love sago pudding for dessert after their dinner. I think that's great, especially as the one I give them is this Thai-inspired version with coconut cream, palm sugar and lime juice. This is a relatively simple dessert: you just need 15 minutes or so to cook the sago before you mix it with the other ingredients, and then at least 4 hours to leave it in the fridge. As far as teaming it with fruit, there are a multitude of choices: mango, banana, lychees or rambutans, paw paw, passionfruit and, my favourite, pineapple. With the fruit you can either make a purée or just simply cut it into fresh pieces, or sugar and roast them, or make them into a coulis. Here I'm giving you the recipe for roasted spiced pineapple.

100 g (3½ oz) palm sugar, chopped

1 star anise

130 g (4½ oz/⅔ cup) sago

3 tablespoons coconut cream

2 teaspoons vanilla extract

2 tablespoons shredded coconut, toasted

SUGAR SYRUP

200 ml (7 fl oz) sugar

200 ml (7 fl oz) water

ROASTED SPICED PINEAPPLE

170 ml (5½ fl oz/⅔ cup) sugar syrup (above)

1 teaspoon grated ginger

200 g (7 oz/1 cup) diced pineapple

To make the sugar syrup, stir the sugar and water in a pan over medium heat until the sugar dissolves.

To make the roasted spiced pineapple, heat the sugar syrup and ginger in a pan until simmering, then add the pineapple and cook for 1 minute. Drain, keeping the liquid. Tip the liquid back into the pan and simmer until thickened. Preheat the oven to 180°C (350°F/Gas 4). Put the pineapple on a baking tray and bake for 20–25 minutes or until starting to caramelise.

Bring 125 ml (4 fl oz/½ cup) of water to the boil in a pan. Add the palm sugar and cook until dissolved. Add the star anise and cook for 5–7 minutes over medium heat or until the syrup has reduced.

Bring a large saucepan of water to the boil and add the sago, stirring to prevent sticking. Simmer for 15 minutes, or until the sago is just transparent. Drain through a sieve and rinse with cold water.

Place the sago in a bowl and stir in the palm sugar mix, coconut cream, vanilla and a pinch of salt. Spoon into ramekins and set in the fridge for 2–4 hours.

Turn out the puddings onto plates and serve with the pineapple, syrup and toasted coconut.

gin punch

serves 4

Punch derives from the early 17th century when it was served from large bowls as the drink of choice in the British colonies. It originally involved a mix of spices, citrus fruit and a measure of spirit. Over time this has progressed to more tropical variations and when you're making it at home you'll find you can include almost anything you want — fruit, spice, herbs and spirits with the trusted citrus to finish.

180 ml (6 fl oz) gin
60 ml (2 fl oz) peach liqueur
360 ml (12 fl oz) ruby red grapefruit juice
3 tablespoons passionfruit pulp
1 tablespoon fresh lime juice
120 ml (4 fl oz) prosecco (Italian sparkling wine)
   or champagne
1 pink grapefruit, sliced

Mix the gin, peach liqueur, grapefruit juice, passionfruit pulp, lime juice and prosecco in a jug.

To serve, fill glasses with ice, pour the punch over the top and serve with pink grapefruit slices.

young raspberry martini

serves 4

This is ideal after dinner with some chocolate mousse, or just as a celebration drink: turn the music up and dance around the house — but watch the raspberries on your cream sofa…

180 ml (6 fl oz) Plymouth gin

60 ml (2 fl oz) raspberry purée (below)

40 ml (1½ fl oz) raspberry syrup (below)

60 ml (2 fl oz) lemon juice

40 ml (1½ fl oz) fresh young coconut juice

1 tablespoon egg white

RASPBERRY PUREE AND SYRUP

100 g (3½ oz) sugar

100 ml (3½ fl oz) water

40 fresh raspberries

To make the raspberry purée and syrup, put the sugar and water in a saucepan and simmer over medium heat, stirring, until dissolved. Add the raspberries and simmer, stirring frequently, until they have broken down and the syrup is fragrant. Pour through a strainer to catch the syrup. Blend the raspberries in a food processor to make the purée.

To make the martinis, pour the gin, raspberry purée, raspberry syrup, lemon juice, coconut juice and egg white into a cocktail shaker. Fill with ice and shake well. Strain finely (twice, if necessary) into chilled martini glasses to serve.

pimm's cooler

serves 4

Pimm's derives from a base of herbs and spices macerated in London Dry Gin. When you're using it as a mixer, try to complement the dark rich notes from the spices with some naturally sweet fruit flavours, such as apple, pear or even ginger beer. Pimms is easy to make in quantity for a party, then left to sit until everyone arrives.

8 orange wedges

1 apple, cut into slices

125 ml (4 fl oz/½ cup) Pimm's

125 ml (4 fl oz/½ cup) gin

250 ml (9 fl oz/1 cup) homemade lemonade (below)

500 ml (17 fl oz/2 cups) sparkling mineral water

12 cucumber slices

16 mint leaves

strawberries and blueberries

HOMEMADE LEMONADE

350 g (12 oz) sugar

500 ml (17 fl oz/2 cups) lemon juice

Put the orange and apple in a jug and add the Pimm's and gin. Leave in the fridge for 2 hours.

To make the lemonade, heat the sugar, lemon juice and 250 ml (9 fl oz/1 cup) of water in a saucepan over low heat, stirring until the sugar has dissolved. Set aside to cool.

Add the lemonade and the sparkling mineral water, to taste. Fill glasses full of ice, pour the drink over and add the cucumber, mint and berries.

mojito

serves 4

2 tablespoons lime juice
8 lime wedges
40 g (1½ oz) sugar
24 mint leaves and 4 mint sprigs
250 ml (9 fl oz/1 cup) Havana Blanco rum
80 ml (2¾ fl oz) soda water
crushed ice

Put the lime juice and wedges, sugar and mint
leaves in a mixing jug and 'muddle' (press down and
crush with a muddler or the end of a rolling pin). Add
the rum, top with soda and fill with crushed ice.
Pour into glasses, stir and top with a sprig of mint.

peach and guava bellini

serves 4

60 ml (2 fl oz) white peach purée
60 ml (2 fl oz) guava juice
1 tablespoon peach liqueur
400 ml (14 fl oz) prosecco (Italian sparkling wine)

Mix together all the ingredients in a large jug and pour into lovely glasses to serve.

The bellini was created by Giuseppe Cipriani at Harry's Bar in Venice. To this day, the bar still pumps out the bellinis *en masse*, but this is an easy mix for any home bartender. Just add 30 ml (1 fl oz) of the nectar or purée of any seasonal fruit to 100 ml (3½ fl oz) of prosecco (a sparkling Italian wine made from white grapes grown in Conegliano, north of Venice).

my indoor table

A croque monsieur is a toasted ham and cheese sandwich that originated in France as a café snack. Everyone has a different method — some put a fried egg on top of the cooked sandwich, others make it with a mustard-flavoured béchamel sauce. I like to keep it simple; use the best-quality leg ham, gruyère cheese, a hint of mustard and lashings of butter. It's not to be eaten every day, but once in a while it makes for a great treat.

croque monsieur

serves 4

butter
8 slices of white bread
2 tablespoons dijon mustard (or your favourite)
100 g (3½ oz) shaved leg ham
100 g (3½ oz) shaved gruyère cheese
8 basil leaves

Preheat the oven to 180°C (350°F/Gas 4). Butter both sides of the bread. Smear one side of four slices with mustard, then top with ham and cheese. Add the basil and season with salt and pepper. Top with another slice of bread to make a sandwich.

Heat a frying pan over medium heat and pan-fry the sandwiches until golden on both sides. Place in the oven to melt the cheese and keep warm while you cook the rest. Cut in half and enjoy.

shakshuka eggs

serves 4

2 green banana chillies
4 large vine-ripened tomatoes, cut into large pieces
3 garlic cloves, chopped
2 teaspoons sweet paprika
3 tablespoons olive oil
4 large free-range eggs
1 large handful of torn coriander (cilantro)
or parsley leaves
4 thick slices of sourdough, toasted

Grill the banana chillies under high heat or over a flame until black and blistered. Put in a plastic bag or cover with a tea towel until cool, to let the skins sweat and loosen. Peel off the blackened skins and scrape out the seeds. Cut the flesh into 1 cm (½ inch) thick strips.

Heat the tomatoes, garlic, paprika, olive oil and some salt in a frying pan. Cover and simmer for 10 minutes, or until the tomatoes have softened. Remove the lid and stir in the chillies. Simmer for a further 8–10 minutes, or until all the juices have evaporated and the sauce is quite thick. Push the sauce to the edge of the pan, leaving space for the eggs to be cracked into.

Break the eggs into the pan, sprinkle with the coriander and season with black pepper. Cover and cook for 3–4 minutes until done to your liking. Serve on toasted sourdough.

Part of my good fortune in being a chef on television is that I have learnt more about food in the last few years than I ever did as an apprentice chef. As an apprentice you spend anywhere from one to four years in a restaurant, working in all the different sections until you are competent. Now with my second career, so to speak, our main focus is on educating the public on the vast array of dishes found all over the globe. So when a recipe like this comes along that I have never heard of, it just blows me away. Michelle, one of the researchers on the show, wanted to cook this Israeli breakfast dish — if you like, jazz it up with some grilled haloumi or merguez sausages.

chocolate waffles

serves 4

1 teaspoon dry yeast

4 tablespoons lukewarm water

1½ tablespoons sugar

250 g (9 oz/2 cups) plain (all-purpose) flour

3 free-range eggs

½ teaspoon vanilla extract

220 g (7 oz/1 cup) Belgian pearl sugar (sometimes called nibbled sugar — or use sugar cubes crushed to about a quarter of their size)

250 g (9 oz/1 cup) softened butter

icing (confectioners') sugar

200 g (7 oz) Callebaut milk chocolate buttons

Combine the yeast, water and sugar and leave for 15 minutes for the yeast to foam and activate.

Place the flour in a large bowl and make a well in the middle. Gently fold in the yeast, then mix in the eggs one at time, followed by the vanilla, pearl sugar and a pinch of salt. Gently knead in the butter for about 5 minutes. The dough should be wet, not sticky and not too dry. Add a little more water or flour if necessary.

Cut the dough into plum-sized balls. Leave to rest and expand for about 15 minutes.

Heat a waffle iron to 200°C (400°F). Cook each waffle for 2 minutes and dust with icing sugar.

Meanwhile, melt the chocolate in a bowl set over a pan of gently simmering water. Stir until melted, then pour over the waffles.

huevos rancheros

serves 4

This is a dish I created about ten years ago with Leela, one of my chefs from Hugo's. Leela was from the United States and we worked the breakfast shift together (my favourite part of the week – organised chaos). She suggested we put huevos rancheros on the menu and I said 'qué?' She patiently explained that it's a tremendously famous Mexican breakfast dish (meaning 'ranchers' eggs') and over the next week or two we came up with the dish as it stands today. This went on to become our biggest breakfast-time seller in Bondi, and I have yet to meet someone who doesn't love it. Thanks Leela; you're a champion!
If you want this hot, splash on a bit of green Tabasco sauce.

2 tablespoons vegetable oil

4 corn tortillas or enchilada tortillas

4 free-range eggs

8 tablespoons refried beans or Mexican beans

8 tablespoons Mexican salsa (your favourite brand)

1 tablespoon chopped coriander (cilantro) leaves

60 g (2 oz/½ cup) grated cheddar cheese

1 avocado, sliced

4 tablespoons sour cream

4 coriander (cilantro) sprigs

1 lime, cut into quarters

12 jalapeño peppers (if you like)

Preheat your grill or oven. Heat the oil in a frying pan and fry the tortillas on both sides until just starting to brown, then place on a baking tray.

Fry your eggs until they are just cooked but the yolks are still soft.

Spread 2 tablespoons of beans over each tortilla. Top with the salsa, place an egg on top of the salsa and season with sea salt and pepper. Sprinkle with the coriander and cheese.

Grill or bake in the oven just until the cheese has melted, then put on plates. Top each serving with avocado slices and a spoonful of sour cream. Garnish with coriander sprigs, and serve with lime wedges and jalapeño peppers.

asparagus with poached egg, nut brown butter and truffled pecorino

serves 4

This is a very impressive dish, which looks fantastic, but takes very little time to put together. It also makes a great dinner for any time you've invited a vegetarian over and then panic about what to cook them. The great thing about this dish is when you break open the poached egg the yolk spills out and mingles with the nut brown butter sauce. Fresh shavings of the best parmesan or truffled pecorino are a must for this, and the addition of some truffle oil or shaved truffle will bring it to another dimension. For an even more impressive dish, try making egg yolk ravioli instead of the poached eggs: simply place an egg yolk between two gow gee wrappers or thin pasta sheets and cook for 45 seconds in boiling salted water.

2 bunches of asparagus

4 free-range eggs

1 teaspoon white wine vinegar

2 tablespoons butter

1 teaspoon crushed garlic

2 teaspoons chopped parsley

a squeeze of lemon juice

crumbled truffled pecorino cheese or
    parmesan shavings

Boil the asparagus in salted water until just tender, then drain. Poach the eggs in just simmering water with the white wine vinegar added.

Heat the butter in a frying pan until it starts to turn brown. Add the garlic, parsley, asparagus, lemon juice and some salt and pepper.

Arrange the asparagus on plates and top with the poached eggs. Drizzle some of the sauce around the plates and over the eggs, then top with the pecorino.

soft-boiled eggs with salmon caviar

serves 4

I love to use salmon caviar on everything from pasta to raw seafood, but my favourite is simply with fresh free-range eggs, either boiled, as here, or scrambled. I was fortunate enough to witness the milking of salmon a few years ago. There is a two-week period each year when they are ready to spawn and it was amazing to watch. The salmon are placed in a clove bath to anaesthetise them, then quickly taken out of the water and gently milked to remove the eggs. Then they're popped back into the water, quite unharmed. The caviar is then blast frozen and defrosted during the year as the market demands.

8 free-range eggs
4 teaspoons salmon roe (or other caviar you like)
8 slices of brioche or sourdough, toasted

Place the eggs in a saucepan of lightly salted water and bring to the boil. Reduce the heat and simmer for 3–4 minutes, then lift out.

Cut the tops off the eggs and season lightly with the salt and pepper. Spoon a teaspoon of salmon roe into each egg. Serve with toasted brioche or sourdough soldiers.

Pumpkin would have to be my favourite soup to eat in winter, and fortunately my kids love it as well. This is a Thai-flavoured pumpkin soup, bursting with those wonderful tastes that Thai food is renowned for... lime, ginger, lemongrass, chilli, kaffir lime and coriander. It is very tasty and easy to make. You can even sprinkle on a few chilli flakes at the end for a burst of heat.

thai pumpkin soup with coconut cream

serves 4

1 tablespoon oil

1 onion, diced

1 lemongrass stem, white part only, finely sliced

1 long red chilli, finely diced

1 tablespoon julienned peeled ginger

1 kaffir lime leaf, julienned

1 bunch of coriander (cilantro), stems and roots
    finely chopped, leaves reserved

3 garlic cloves, finely chopped

1 kg (2 lb 4 oz) pumpkin, peeled and cut into cubes

270 ml (9½ fl oz) coconut cream

270 ml (9½ fl oz) coconut milk

500 ml (17 fl oz/2 cups) vegetable stock

zest of 1 orange

Heat the oil in a saucepan over medium heat and add the onion, lemongrass, chilli, ginger, kaffir lime, coriander stems and roots, and garlic. Fry until the flavours start to release but stop before it turns brown. Add the pumpkin, half the coconut cream, the coconut milk, vegetable stock and orange zest.

Cook for about 30 minutes, or until the pumpkin is tender. Blend in a food processor and pass through a strainer if you want it extra smooth.

Season with salt and cracked white pepper and serve with the coriander leaves and the rest of the coconut cream swirled through it.

This is a special-occasion recipe for me; it is a classic that has stood the test of time and probably the one offal dish that most people like. There are a couple of different methods to making pâté or parfait. A pâté is when the livers are cooked in the pan and then blended and set with butter; while for a parfait, raw ingredients are blended together and then cooked slowly in a tin in a water bath. I have opted for a pâté recipe, as I like to be able to check I'm not overcooking the livers and, even more importantly, because I love the intoxicating aroma that fills the kitchen when I cook them. You can serve pâté with any type of bread — fresh crusty chunks torn off the loaf, or toasted sourdough — but my all-time favourite is buttery warm, delicately toasted brioche that melts in the mouth.

duck liver pâté with toasted brioche

Makes enough for 1 loaf of bread or a large party of people

50 g (1¾ oz) clarified butter, for frying livers

500 g (1 lb 2 oz) duck livers (soaked in 200 ml/
    7 fl oz milk for 2 hours, then strained)

3 garlic cloves, finely chopped

2 French shallots, finely chopped

1½ tablespoons chopped thyme

60 ml (2 fl oz/¼ cup) brandy

60 ml (2 fl oz/¼ cup) port

60 ml (2 fl oz/¼ cup) Madeira

1½ tablespoons dijon mustard

325 g (11½ oz) butter, at room temperature

1 free-range egg yolk

serve with brioche and condiments such as
    cornichons, pickled onions, sour cherries, caper
    berries and sweet and sour onions (page 144)

Melt some of the clarified butter in a frying pan over medium heat and fry the livers in batches until just rare, wiping out the pan between batches, and repeat the process. Remove from the pan.

Add the garlic, shallots and thyme to the pan and sauté until transparent, then add the alcohol and flame to reduce to a honey consistency. Transfer to a blender and purée until smooth. Add the livers and mustard and purée until smooth. Add the butter gradually and season with salt and pepper. Add the egg yolk and blend until smooth, then pass through a strainer. Spoon into ramekins or a large terrine mould lined with plastic wrap, and leave to set in the fridge for 4 hours, or overnight.

brioche

500 g (1 lb 2 oz) strong baker's flour

2 teaspoons salt

1 tablespoon sugar

6 large free-range eggs

22 g (¾ oz) fresh yeast

60 g (2 oz) butter, softened and diced

1 free-range egg, extra, lightly beaten, to glaze

Put the flour, salt and sugar in a mixing bowl. Using an electric mixer with a dough hook attachment, start the mixer on low speed and add the eggs one at a time. Add the yeast and continue to mix for 2–3 minutes. Add the butter, a piece at a time, and continue mixing for another 8 minutes. The dough should be smooth and elastic. Put in a large oiled bowl, cover with plastic wrap and leave in the fridge overnight.

Knock back the dough on a lightly floured work surface. Divide into two portions, shape and place on oiled baking trays or in two greased loaf tins and leave to prove until doubled in size. Preheat the oven to 180°C (350°F/Gas 4). Brush the top with egg and bake for 20–30 minutes, or until golden.

stracciatella soup with cavolo nero and lardo

serves 4

Stracciatella is a classic Roman egg-drop soup that loosely translates as 'little rags' (because when you whisk the egg and parmesan into the hot broth it looks like torn rags). I have taken the liberty of adding some cavolo nero for texture and also some lardo for added flavour. If you want to make a meal out of this dish, just add some small risoni pasta and shredded roast chicken.

1 litre (35 fl oz/4 cups) chicken stock

100 g (3½ oz) cavolo nero (dark Italian cabbage)
    or spinach

4 free-range eggs

75 g (2½ oz/¾ cup) grated parmesan

2 teaspoons lemon juice

4 tablespoons chopped parsley

12 thin slices of lardo (cured pork fat), if you like,
    or extra virgin olive oil, to drizzle

Bring the chicken stock to the boil in a saucepan. Blanch the cavolo nero in the stock for 30 seconds, then take out and roughly chop.

Beat the eggs, parmesan, lemon and parsley together with a fork. Pour into the stock and stir for 1 minute, then add the cavolo nero and season with salt and pepper. Serve topped with the lardo or olive oil.

steak tartare

serves 4

400 g (14 oz) eye fillet of beef

2 tablespoons dijon mustard

4 anchovy fillets, finely chopped

2 tablespoons tomato sauce (ketchup)

1 tablespoon worcestershire sauce

Tabasco sauce, to taste

3 tablespoons extra virgin olive oil

1½ tablespoons cognac (if you like)

4 tablespoons finely chopped red onion

60 g (2 oz) capers, rinsed

60 g (2 oz) cornichons, finely chopped

1 small handful of parsley, finely chopped

4 free-range egg yolks

french fries or croûtes, to serve

Chop the meat very finely with a sharp knife.

Mix the mustard and anchovies in a large stainless steel bowl. Add the tomato sauce, worcestershire sauce, Tabasco and some pepper and mix well. Slowly whisk in the oil, and then the cognac. Fold in the onion, capers, cornichons, parsley and a little salt.

Add the meat to the bowl and mix well with a spoon or your hands. Serve on plates, using a ring mould to shape the meat into neat circles. Make a small hollow on the top of each one with a spoon and place an egg yolk in it. Sprinkle with sea salt and cracked pepper. Serve with fries or croûtes.

One of the most memorable things about travelling through France was the food I ate… delicious meals of duck, foie gras, pâté, soufflés. But the thing that stood out the most for me was the simple and tasty steak tartare. The amount they served up was enough to stop a grown man in his tracks: I have never seen so much raw beef on a plate, let alone my own. Sometimes they teamed this with *pommes frîtes* (French fries), which actually works a treat. I like to serve it at home as a small entrée, so that you are still wanting more when the last mouthful goes in. I have given the traditional French preparation here as I don't think there is any need to mess with such a classic, however, if you do want to be adventurous, a little truffle paste or oil mixed through will take this favourite to another dimension.

wild mushroom risotto soup

serves 4

What I just love about a recipe like this is how quick and easy it is to make for a group of people, and what very little chance there is of stuffing it up! This is a very wet risotto that is meant to be eaten more like a soup than a rice dish. It is beautiful in autumn when the wild mushrooms, such as pines or slippery jacks, are in season.

160 ml (5 fl oz) veal stock

160 g (5¾ oz) arborio rice

800 ml (28 fl oz/3¼ cups) chicken or vegetable stock
   or water

2 tablespoons olive oil

250 g (9 oz) assorted mushrooms, such as pine,
   porcini, enoki, swiss brown, shiitake

2 garlic cloves, chopped

2 tablespoons chopped parsley

1 teaspoon lemon juice

freshly grated Parmigiano Reggiano

Heat the veal stock in a saucepan over medium heat until reduced by half.

Wash the rice under cold running water to remove the starch. Place in a saucepan, add the chicken or vegetable stock and bring to a simmer. Simmer for about 20 minutes until the rice is cooked, season, then add extra stock or water if needed.

Meanwhile, heat the oil in a frying pan and cook the mushrooms until golden. Add the garlic and parsley and cook for 30 seconds, then add the lemon juice.

Add half the mushrooms to the soup, pour into bowls and top with the rest of the mushrooms. Spoon a little veal stock over the soup and serve with the grated parmesan.

good old-fashioned prawns with cocktail sauce

serves 4–6

I love prawns. I reckon I could write a whole bloody book about prawns. Barbecued prawns, crumbed prawns, battered prawns, steamed prawns, pan-fried prawns, grilled prawns, boiled prawns, raw sashimi-style prawns, curried prawns, prawn cocktails, prawn sandwiches, prawn… you get the picture. They would have to be the most versatile seafood and the one people love the most. Let's start with the simplest way to prepare them — and the one everyone orders from the seafood shops — cooked prawns. On the trawlers they have vats for cooking the prawns immediately after harvesting, then they are snap-chilled to retain their freshness. The way I like to cook prawns is to steam them — I think if you boil them you actually lose some of the flavour. You can serve them with some fresh lemon, but I love them with a good old-fashioned cocktail sauce.

1.5 kg (3 lb 5 oz/about 30) raw king prawns

1 free-range egg

a dash of Tabasco

1 tablespoon dijon mustard

2 tablespoons worcestershire sauce

4 tablespoons tomato sauce (ketchup)

1–2 tablespoons sea salt

juice of 1 lemon

500 ml (17 fl oz/2 cups) grapeseed oil

Cook the prawns in a steamer over boiling water for about 4–7 minutes (depending on their size) until they are pink/orange and firm to the touch. Peel, devein and put the prawns in a bowl. Cover with plastic wrap and leave in the fridge until you are ready to serve.

Meanwhile, combine the egg, Tabasco, mustard, worcestershire and tomato sauces, salt and lemon juice. Blend with a stick blender, then slowly add the oil. Season and serve with the cold prawns (you can store any leftover sauce in a sealed jar in the fridge).

scallops with ginger and spring onions

serves 4

I absolutely love scallops, and this is a classic recipe that hits all the right notes. It is flavoursome but does not overpower the scallops and is still very light. This is a great dish to serve as an entrée or to make into a big party platter. You can use oysters instead of the scallops if you like, or go wild and serve both.

16 scallops on the half shell

1 knob of ginger, julienned

2 spring onions (scallions), finely shredded (keep the white and green parts separate)

125 ml (4 fl oz/½ cup) mirin or shaoxing wine

3 tablespoons light soy sauce

2 tablespoons rice wine vinegar

2 teaspoons sugar

3 tablespoons peanut oil or grapeseed oil

Lay the scallops in a steamer basket with the ginger and white part of the spring onions and some white pepper and steam for a few minutes.

Stir the mirin, soy sauce, vinegar and sugar in a pan over medium heat until the sugar dissolves.

Heat the oil in a saucepan until smoking. Arrange the scallops on a platter and spoon the hot oil over them. Spoon the dressing over the top and garnish with the green spring onions.

fried oysters with sweet and sour onions

serves 4

POOR MAN'S PARMESAN AÏOLI

2 tablespoons fresh breadcrumbs

1 anchovy, drained and chopped

1 tablespoon chopped flat-leaf (Italian) parsley

1 teaspoon olive oil

4 tablespoons aïoli (page 40)

SWEET AND SOUR ONIONS

2 tablespoons olive oil

1 large onion, thinly sliced

2 tablespoons sugar

2 tablespoons balsamic vinegar

500 ml (17 fl oz/2 cups) peanut oil

24 oysters (Sydney rock, Pacific or Angassi)

flour, for dusting

½ quantity of tempura batter (opposite)

To make the poor man's parmesan aïoli, preheat the oven to 150°C (300°F/Gas 2). Mix the breadcrumbs, anchovy, parsley and olive oil, spread over a baking tray lined with baking paper and bake for 10 minutes, or until dry. Grind with a mortar and pestle, leaving the mixture a little coarse. Mix with the aïoli.

To make the sweet and sour onions, heat the oil in a pan and cook the onion, stirring, until just starting to colour. Add the sugar and balsamic and simmer until reduced almost to a jam consistency. Season to taste with salt and serve warm or chilled.

Heat the peanut oil to 185°C (350°F) in a wok or deep frying pan.

Remove the oysters from their shells. Dust lightly in flour and shake off the excess, then dip the oysters in the tempura batter and drain off any excess.

Lower the oysters into the wok and cook until crisp and golden. Drain on kitchen paper. Put back on their shells to serve with sweet and sour onions and the poor man's parmesan aïoli.

In the cooler months the Pacific oysters out of Tassie and South Australia, as well as the Sydney rock oysters from the south coast of NSW, are at their best. However, sometimes you don't want to eat oysters *au naturel* when it's chilly outside. This recipe is perfect for those times and any leftover sweet and sour onions can be used in your next steak sandwich or with a roast pork dinner. For something different, I have teamed the oysters with what is known as poor man's parmesan aïoli, which is basically flavoured breadcrumbs. It is said that when you ran out of parmesan, or couldn't afford to buy it, this was the substitute. It is also delicious sprinkled over pasta instead of parmesan, especially seafood pastas.

fried zucchini flowers with salsa verde

serves 4

Zucchini flowers are the golden blossoms of baby zucchini and are generally available in spring and summer. This preparation is a classic and it is how I serve them at home as an entrée when I have guests coming round. Keep the dusting of batter very light and always drain them well after frying. You can serve the salsa verde on the side in a bowl to dip into or drizzle it over the whole plateful of zucchini flowers. For something a bit more indulgent, try filling the flowers with some mud crab or even salted cod brandade. If you want to keep it vegetarian, try goat's cheese, ricotta or, my personal favourite, although not vegetarian, is creamy Italian buffalo milk mozzarella and an anchovy... heaven.

Oh, and if you can't find zucchini flowers, no need to worry... just cut an ordinary zucchini into batons and cook the same way.

SALSA VERDE

1 slice of stale bread

250 ml (9 fl oz/1 cup) olive oil

100 g (3½ oz/2 cups) basil leaves

100 g (3½ oz/2 cups) flat-leaf (Italian) parsley

4 anchovies

50 g (1¾ oz) capers

1 tablespoon finely chopped cornichons

1 tablespoon lemon juice

50 g (1¾ oz) pine nuts, toasted

TEMPURA BATTER

150 g (5½ oz/1¼ cups) tempura or plain flour

350 ml (12 fl oz) cold sparkling mineral water

1 handful of ice cubes

16 zucchini (courgette) flowers

flour, for dusting

1 litre (35 fl oz/4 cups) vegetable oil, for deep-frying

lemon wedges, to serve

To make the salsa verde, soak the bread in the oil for 5 minutes. Mix all the ingredients in a blender and season with salt and pepper. Keep in a sterilised jar in the fridge.

To make the tempura batter, mix the flour and mineral water so it looks like cream, then add the ice cubes.

Inside the zucchini flowers are the stamen (male) or pistils (female) — remove these with tweezers or with your fingers (not really necessary but they will taste better if you do this).

Heat the oil to 185°C (350°F) in a wok or deep frying pan. Lightly dust the flowers in flour and shake off the excess. Dip in the tempura batter and drain off the excess. Deep-fry for about 2 minutes until the flowers are lightly golden and crisp. Drain on kitchen paper and sprinkle with sea salt. Serve with lemon wedges and salsa verde.

gnocchi with cotechino sausage

serves 4

250 g (9 oz) cotechino sausage

1 tablespoon olive oil

1 quantity of Italian tomato sauce (right)

1 handful of basil leaves, torn

grated parmesan, to serve

POTATO GNOCCHI

600 g (1 lb 5 oz) desiree potatoes, unpeeled

30 g (1 oz) unsalted butter, softened

30 g (1 oz) parmesan, grated

1 free-range egg yolk

10 g (½ oz) sea salt

60 g (2 oz) '00' flour

semolina, for dusting

Gently simmer the cotechino in water for 2 hours, then cool and cut into 5 mm (¼ inch) thick slices.

To make the gnocchi, simmer the potatoes in salted water until cooked through. Drain, peel and dry out in a hot pan for a minute.

Purée the potatoes with a mouli or ricer. Transfer to a mixer with a paddle blade on low speed and add the butter, parmesan, egg yolk and salt. Add the flour until the dough doesn't stick to your fingers. Roll out into 1 cm (½ inch) thick logs on a work surface dusted with semolina. Cut at 3 cm (1 inch) intervals, then blanch in a large saucepan of gently boiling salted water until they float to the surface. Lift out with a slotted spoon.

Heat the olive oil in a frying pan and cook the cotechino until starting to colour, then turn and cook for a further minute. Add the tomato sauce and bring to a simmer. Season with salt and pepper and add the basil leaves. Add the gnocchi and lightly stir to coat in the sauce. Serve with grated parmesan.

NOTE If you can't find cotechino, use fresh Italian pork sausage. Don't boil it like the cotechino — pan-fry like normal sausage and break into pieces.

Italian tomato sauce

2 tablespoons olive oil

50 g (1¾ oz) garlic, thinly sliced

500 g (1 lb 2 oz) tinned tomatoes, crushed

8 basil leaves

Heat the oil in a saucepan and cook the garlic until it's starting to colour. Add the tomatoes and 125 ml (4 fl oz/½ cup) of water and simmer for 20–25 minutes. Add the basil and cook for another 5 minutes. Season to taste and blend until smooth.

rocket, pear and walnut salad with blue cheese dressing

serves 4

Rocket salads are very easy to throw together and suit most Mediterranean dishes. The simplest versions are rocket, parmesan, olive oil and either lemon juice or balsamic vinegar — job done. If you want to add another dimension, try this simple dressing with blue cheese to complement the pear and walnuts.

BLUE CHEESE DRESSING

1 teaspoon dijon mustard

1 tablespoon white wine vinegar

½ tablespoon lemon juice

125 ml (4 fl oz/½ cup) extra virgin olive oil

1 tablespoon softened blue cheese

125 g (4½ oz) baby rocket

20 thin slices of unpeeled pear

40 g (1½ oz/⅓ cup) roasted walnuts, roughly chopped

2 tablespoons crumbled blue cheese

To make the dressing, whisk the ingredients together thoroughly.

Put the rocket, pear, walnuts and half of the dressing in a large bowl and toss lightly. Add the blue cheese, and taste to see whether to add the rest of the dressing.

tomato and ricotta tortellini with basil

serves 4

This is a recipe from my Hugo's Bondi days. It was on our first menu and actually stayed there for years as our vegetarian main course. It wasn't ordered only by the vegetarians presumably, as it turned out to be one of our best sellers. It's a dish which goes to prove that good food doesn't have to cost an arm and a leg, or take hours to prepare. You can make this even more speedy if you buy oven-roasted tomatoes from the deli, and pre-rolled fresh lasagne sheets if you don't have a pasta machine at home or just can't be bothered.

TOMATO AND RICOTTA FILLING

250 g (9 oz/1 cup) ricotta cheese

40 g (1½ oz/¼ cup) semi-dried tomatoes,
    finely chopped

1 free-range egg yolk

6 basil leaves, finely sliced

1 tablespoon grated Parmigiano Reggiano

1–2 tablespoons tomato juice (if you like)

1 tablespoon extra virgin olive oil

8 fresh lasagne sheets or 40 gow gee wrappers

1 free-range egg, lightly beaten

125 g (4½ oz) butter

1 tablespoon lemon juice

1 tablespoon extra virgin olive oil

8 basil leaves

8 red basil leaves

14 cherry tomatoes, halved and dried in a very low
    oven (or use fresh)

1 garlic clove, crushed

1 tablespoon grated Parmigiano Reggiano, plus
    some to serve

To make the filling, mix together all the ingredients. Place the lasagne sheets on a bench and cut into 9 cm (3½ inch) squares. Using a pastry brush, wet the edges of each square with beaten egg.

Place 1 tablespoon of filling in the centre of each pasta square and fold over diagonally to make a triangle. Brush a little more egg on two corners of each triangle and twist around your fingers so they come together. Press together to seal.

Cook the tortellini in boiling salted water for about 2 minutes or until cooked through, then lift out with a slotted spoon.

Heat the butter in a frying pan for 2–3 minutes until it turns nut brown. Remove from the heat and add the lemon juice and olive oil. Add the basil, cherry tomatoes, garlic, tortellini and parmesan and toss gently. Serve with some more parmesan over the top.

hot pepperoni pizza with mint and buffalo milk mozzarella

makes enough for four 30 cm (12 inch) pizza bases

As you may know, I own a restaurant called Hugo's Bar Pizza in Kings Cross and also one in Sydney's Manly. Hugo's specialises in pizza, Italian food and great cocktails. When I was designing the pizzas for the menu, I wanted a pepperoni pizza on there — it's my favourite type of pizza, hands down — but I wanted to give it a twist on the ones you would order from your local pizzeria. For one, we started off with very hot salami, and then I read that in Italy they sometimes team mint with chilli to counteract the heat and thus create a beautiful marriage. So this is where the unusual combination of mint leaves and hot pepperoni came into play. Team that pair up with some creamy buffalo mozzarella and you have something worthy of an Italian opera happening in your mouth. If you can't get your hands on some good-quality hot salami, just try sprinkling hot dried chilli flakes over the pizza once it is cooked.

1 quantity of pizza dough, opposite

8 garlic cloves, roasted and crushed

2 tablespoons extra virgin olive oil

½ quantity of tomato pizza sauce (opposite)

160 g (5¾ oz) mozzarella, shredded

2 punnets of cherry tomatoes, cut into thirds

1 small handful of chopped flat-leaf (Italian) Italian parsley

300 g (10 oz) hot pepperoni or salami, sliced paper thin

chilli flakes, to taste

2 handfuls of mint leaves

1 ball of buffalo mozzarella, torn into pieces

Preheat your oven to its highest temperature. Divide the dough into four portions and roll out on a lightly floured surface until you have four thin pizza bases. Place on baking trays and prick the bases all over with a fork to stop air bubbles forming when they are cooking.

Combine the garlic with the olive oil.

Spread the pizza bases with the tomato sauce, then top with the mozzarella, cherry tomatoes, garlic oil, parsley, pepperoni, chilli flakes and some salt.

Bake the pizzas for 5–10 minutes, or until crisp. Top with the mint leaves and buffalo mozzarella.

pizza dough

3 teaspoons dry yeast
3 teaspoons sugar
3 teaspoons salt
1 tablespoon olive oil
425 g (15 oz) 00 (bakers') flour

To make the dough, put the yeast, sugar, salt and olive oil in a mixing bowl with 250 ml (9 fl oz/1 cup) of warm water and stir gently. Leave for 15 minutes for the yeast to activate (it will look foamy). Add the flour slowly and knead for about 5 minutes until the dough is smooth.

Put in a lightly oiled bowl and leave in a warm place for about 30 minutes to an hour until doubled in size, then knock back with one good punch. Leave in a warm place until it has risen slightly.

Makes enough for four 30 cm (12 inch) pizzas.

tomato pizza sauce

400 g (14 oz) tinned tomatoes
a pinch of sea salt
a pinch of black peppercorns
a pinch of dried oregano

To make the tomato sauce, blend the tomatoes, salt, peppercorns and oregano in a food processor.

Makes 2 cupfuls of tomato sauce (enough for about eight pizzas). Can be frozen.

italian meatballs

serves 4

350 g (12 oz) pork mince

150 g (5½ oz) veal mince

100 g (3½ oz) parmesan, grated

80 g (2¾ oz/1 cup) fresh breadcrumbs

2 tablespoons chopped parsley

2 free-range egg yolks

2 tablespoons olive oil

500 ml (17 fl oz/2 cups) Italian tomato sauce
    (page 148)

shaved pecorino cheese, to serve

Preheat the oven to 180°C (350°F/Gas 4). Mix together the pork, veal, parmesan, breadcrumbs, parsley, egg yolks and some salt and pepper. Roll into golf ball-sized balls.

Heat the oil in an ovenproof frying pan and fry the meatballs until golden on one side, then turn over and place in the oven for 5 minutes until cooked.

Add the tomato sauce to the pan and heat through on the stove top, then serve with the pecorino cheese.

The Italians have a wonderful approach to cooking, which is why so many of their dishes become staples in our own homes — even when we're not Italian! I've just finished reading a wonderful book called *The Food of Love* by Anthony Capella, who talks about food not only as a source of enjoyment but also as a means of transforming people's different emotional states. The dish I love to prepare, and the one which makes my daughters go crazy and chant 'more please, Daddy', would have to be Italian meatballs. The sheer simplicity of this is the key to its appeal, which will continue to appeal as time goes by. You could add your favourite pasta to this, or better still, sandwich the tomatoey meatballs in a bread roll for a great lunch. It certainly transforms my emotional state…

mum's spaghetti bolognese

serves 4

There is only one thing that needs to be said here: my mum makes the best spaghetti bolognese in the world. Love you mum!

2 tablespoons olive oil

½ onion, finely chopped

3 garlic cloves, finely chopped

500 g (1 lb 2 oz) minced beef

1 teaspoon dried oregano

250 ml (9 fl oz/1 cup) red wine (I use a shiraz)

2 tablespoons tomato paste

3 tablespoons tomato sauce (ketchup)

1 tablespoon sweet chilli sauce or a pinch
   of chilli flakes

400 g (14 oz) tin tomato soup

250 ml (9 fl oz/1 cup) chicken stock

cooked spaghetti (fresh pasta preferably)

4 tablespoons chopped flat-leaf (Italian) parsley

Parmigiano Reggiano, grated

silverbeet, mushrooms, zucchini (optional — this is
   what mum likes to add to the sauce to make it
   a bit healthier, but I'm not really into it...
   sorry mum)

Heat the oil in a large frying pan. Add the onion and garlic and cook until soft. Add the mince and brown for 3–4 minutes. Add the oregano and wine and cook until almost evaporated.

Add the tomato paste and sauces and cook for 1 minute. Add the soup, half the chicken stock and a good touch of salt and black pepper. Simmer for 30 minutes (adding the rest of the stock if needed).

Add the hot pasta and parsley and toss through. Sprinkle with grated parmesan and enjoy with the rest of the shiraz.

quick italian seafood stew

serves 4

Seafood is a very good friend to me and my family. We even base family holidays around it — going to fish in different destinations around Australia and overseas with friends. We either eat our catch there and then, or bring it home frozen so that we can pull it out of the freezer later to remind us what a great time we had (other people do this with wines, but I find fishing memories much more exciting). This is a quick and easy seafood dish that gives you plenty of essential omega 3s, and will bring back great memories if you've caught the fish yourself.

4 tablespoons olive oil

1 onion, thinly sliced

2 garlic cloves, crushed

a pinch of saffron

1 teaspoon of chilli flakes (if you like)

170 ml (5½ fl oz/⅔ cup) white wine

2 tablespoons tomato paste

400 g (14 oz) tinned tomatoes, crushed

375ml (13 fl oz/1½ cups) fish stock

300 g (10½ oz) firm white fish, cut into pieces

8 mussels, cleaned

400 g (14 oz) raw king prawns, peeled and
        deveined, tails intact

8 scallops

2 tablespoons chopped parsley

GARLIC AND HERB BREAD

150 g (5½ oz) butter, softened

3 garlic cloves, crushed

1 tablespoon finely chopped basil

1 tablespoon finely chopped parsley

1 tablespoon finely chopped chervil

2 tablespoons finely grated parmesan

½ French bread stick, thickly sliced

Heat the oil in a large saucepan and cook the onion for 1 minute until softened. Add the garlic, saffron, chilli and wine and simmer for 2 minutes. Add the tomato paste, tomatoes and stock, then cover and cook for 20–25 minutes.

Season with salt and pepper, then add the fish, mussels, prawns and scallops. Cook for a further 5 minutes and stir in the chopped parsley. Serve with garlic and herb bread.

To make the garlic and herb bread, mix the butter thoroughly with the garlic, basil, parsley, chervil and parmesan and season with salt and pepper. Grill the bread slices on one side only, then spread thickly with the garlic herb butter. Return to the grill and cook for 1–2 minutes or until lightly browned.

My favourite dish that gets cooked for me at home is this one right here: Astrid's spinach pie. Astrid is my partner and when she gets into the kitchen you gotta stand back… she is one of those cooks who gets extremely uptight because she wants everything to be perfect. This is quite the opposite of me — I don't mind mistakes and I don't get too caught up when I'm cooking. In fact, after cooking for a hundred people a night in the restaurant, I find it relaxing to make food at home. This is a crowd favourite, especially good because the kids love it too, which is a great way of getting spinach into their diet. I like to eat my pie with some chilli jam on the side, which shocks Astrid as she's a purist and just loves a simple squeeze of lemon.

astrid's spinach and feta pie with chilli jam

serves 4

1 bunch of silverbeet

250 g (9 oz) English spinach

1 bunch of chives, finely chopped

½ bunch of dill, finely chopped

250 g (9 oz) cottage cheese

250 g (9 oz) feta cheese, crumbled

3 free-range eggs

1 teaspoon dried oregano, preferably Greek

2 sheets frozen puff pastry, thawed

1 free-range egg, lightly beaten, to glaze

1 lemon, cut into quarters

Preheat the oven to 220°C (425°F/Gas 7). Cut the thick woody stalks from the silverbeet and spinach. Blanch for 2 minutes in boiling salted water. Drain, run under cold water, then wring out any excess water in a tea towel. Chop very finely and mix with the chives, dill, cottage cheese, feta, eggs, dried oregano and some salt and pepper.

Roll out one sheet of puff pastry on a floured surface to 35 x 25 cm (14 x 10 inches). Grease a 27 x 17 cm (10¾ x 6½ inch) baking tin and line with one sheet of pastry, letting it go up the sides. Spread the filling over the pastry, then roll out the other pastry sheet to 27 x 25 (10¾ x 10 inches) to cover. Trim and pinch the pastry edges together. Brush the pie with egg. Bake for 15 minutes until golden, then reduce the heat to 200°C (400°F/Gas 6) and cook for another 15–20 minutes until cooked through. Serve with lemon and chilli jam.

chilli jam

1 tablespoon olive oil

1 red onion, diced

1 red capsicum (pepper), chopped

1 punnet of cherry tomatoes

10 long red chillies, deseeded and chopped

2 tablespoons chopped coriander (cilantro) root and stem

115 g (4 oz/½ cup) soft brown sugar

2 tablespoons sambal oelek

1–2 tablespoons fish sauce

1 lemon, peeled and chopped, pips removed

Heat the oil in a pan and fry the onion and capsicum until soft. Add the remaining ingredients and simmer for 30 minutes. Blend until smooth and then season.

spinach, goat's cheese and pesto salad

serves 4

I have been making a version of this salad in my restaurants for over fifteen years now and it's a sure crowd-pleaser. You need perfect un-bruised spinach leaves for this simple recipe. I love the addition of some creamy goat's curd (not hard goat's cheese) and also the surprising flavour you get from stirring crushed roasted hazelnuts through the pesto. This is great as a salad to go with a roast dinner or, better still, cook a lamb back strap or rump, let it rest, then slice and toss through the salad to make a main meal.

200 g (7 oz) baby English spinach leaves

¼ red onion, finely diced

5 tablespoons extra virgin olive oil

2 tablespoons balsamic vinegar

4–6 tablespoons soft goat's curd (chèvre)

2 tablespoons crushed roasted hazelnuts

pesto

2 garlic cloves, roasted and peeled

2 tablespoons toasted pine nuts

1 anchovy (if you like)

100 g (3½ oz/2 cups) basil leaves

2 tablespoons grated parmesan

zest and juice of 1 lemon

200 ml (7 fl oz) olive oil

To make the pesto, either using a mortar and pestle or hand blender, pound the garlic to a paste with some sea salt, add the pine nuts and then the anchovy, pounding all the time. Next, pound in the basil and then the cheese, then the lemon zest, lemon juice and olive oil until it has a sauce consistency. Season with black pepper.

Lightly toss the spinach leaves with the red onion and some sea salt and pepper. Add the oil and vinegar, gently toss again and arrange the goat's curd on top.

Mix the roasted hazelnuts with 4 tablespoons of pesto and drizzle over the top of the salad (keep any leftover pesto in a screw-top jar in the fridge, covering the surface with a layer of oil).

pappardelle with rabbit ragù

serves 4

I know a lot of young people might not appreciate rabbit as much as the older generation do, but give this a go and it will definitely change your mind. This is a great preparation; very simple and very comforting. The main component is the rabbit ragù, with which you can do pretty much anything you want — put it through a risotto, serve it with mashed potatoes, toss it through some gnocchi or pop it on toasted brioche. For this recipe I've teamed it with pasta, but if you have any leftover you can fill ravioli with it and serve with a brown butter sauce with sage leaves and roasted chestnuts — a great winter warmer. You can make this recipe with goat, duck, pigeon — pretty much any game you like.

2 tablespoons olive oil

1 whole cleaned rabbit, cut into pieces

60 g (2 oz) diced carrot

60 g (2 oz) diced celery

60 g (2 oz) diced onion

60 g (2 oz) diced pancetta

60 g (2 oz) chopped parsley

200 ml (7 fl oz) red wine

400 ml (14 fl oz) veal stock

500 g (1 lb 2 oz) tinned tomatoes, crushed

600 g (1 lb 5 oz) pappardelle

100 g (3½ oz) fresh peas

grated parmesan, to serve

Preheat the oven to 150°C (300°F/Gas 2).

Heat the oil in a large casserole dish over medium heat and brown the rabbit pieces until golden. Remove from the casserole.

Add more oil to the dish and sauté the diced vegetables and pancetta until translucent. Add the rabbit pieces and parsley. Add the red wine and bring to a simmer. Add the stock and tomatoes and cover, then place in the oven for about 2 hours.

Take all the rabbit meat off the bone and keep on one side for now. Put the dish on the stove top and cook, uncovered, over medium heat until the sauce has thickened. Return the rabbit to the sauce.

Meanwhile, cook the pasta and peas together in boiling salted water and then drain. Toss through the rabbit sauce and serve with parmesan.

chilli prawns with snow peas

serves 4

3 tablespoons grapeseed oil

1 kg (2 lb 4 oz) raw king prawns, peeled and
deveined

3 small white spring onions (scallions), thinly sliced

8 garlic cloves, thinly sliced

1 red bird's eye chilli, finely chopped

170 ml (5½ fl oz/⅔ cup) chilli sauce

100 g (3½ oz) snow peas (mangetout), trimmed

1 small handful of coriander (cilantro) leaves

steamed rice, to serve

Heat a touch of the grapeseed oil in a wok and cook the prawns in batches for about 30 seconds on each side or until pink and just cooked through. Remove them all from the wok, set aside on a warm plate and sprinkle with a touch of sea salt.

Add the remaining oil to the wok and cook the spring onion, garlic and chilli for about 30 seconds. Add the chilli sauce and snow peas and cook until just heated through (be careful not to overcook the snow peas — they should still be crunchy). Return the prawns to the wok, toss together and scatter with coriander. Serve with steamed rice.

cherry tomato pasta

serves 4

I cook this more than any other meal at home for my family. (I never cook it for my friends in case they think I'm completely lacking in imagination!) But as they say, 'you never know what goes on behind closed doors', and this is what goes on behind mine... a simple pasta dish that has just a few ingredients: cherry tomatoes, garlic (lots of it), chilli, anchovies and fresh herbs — I tend to alternate between basil and parsley. If I'm using parsley I fry it into the sauce at the start, but I tear the basil into the pasta at the last minute. Sometimes I pop capers or olives in here, or finish it with rocket or spinach and a squeeze of lemon. You can also make it with a fresh, uncooked tomato sauce: just making a dressing, crush the cherry tomatoes with a potato masher and add basil and cooked pasta for a light summer lunch. It is one of those dishes that changes every time I cook it — perhaps that's exactly what I love about it.

150 ml (5½ fl oz) extra virgin olive oil

10 garlic cloves, thinly sliced

2 bird's eye chillies, finely chopped

6 anchovies

1 tablespoon capers

2 punnets of cherry tomatoes, halved

2 tablespoons white wine

1 small handful of basil leaves

400 g (14 oz) orecchiette or any pasta you like

juice of ½ lemon

shaved Parmigiano Reggiano, to serve

Combine the oil, garlic, chilli and anchovies in a pan over medium–low heat until the garlic starts to turn a light brown colour. Break down the anchovies with a wooden spoon.

Add the capers, tomatoes and white wine and season with salt and pepper. Cook for another 3 minutes, then stir in the basil.

Meanwhile, cook the pasta in boiling salted water according to the packet instructions, then drain. Add to the sauce and toss well. Stir in the lemon juice and serve with the shaved parmesan.

I love simple recipes and I don't mind using sauces straight from the bottle from time to time — in fact, I think they're absolutely terrific for the times you don't have half an hour to make your own sauce. The most important thing to remember is to use the freshest possible prawns you can get your hands on (you could use frozen ones, but make sure you use them the day of defrosting). The rest is as simple as ABC.

My Christmas day ritual is to get up early and go surfing, usually with my brother Dave. Chrissy day is one of the most uncrowded times in the waves as everyone is at home opening their presents. Because of this early morning escape, and the fact that I'm always blessed with doing the cooking honours for the day (slave, in other words), I like to make it all as painless and indulgent as possible. Hence my baked Christmas ham. This can be cooked a day in advance and it actually tastes better the next day. The recipe was handed to me by a very good friend of mine, Rob Vandyke, stepfather of Maddie Hayes, one of the best apprentices I've ever had. Sadly, Rob passed away last year... but his memory will live on in our hearts and his superb ham will be forever on my Christmas table.

rob's christmas ham with fennel coleslaw

serves 4

500 g (1 lb 2 oz) apricot jam

185 ml (6 fl oz/¾ cup) dry sherry

1 large cooked cold leg of ham

1 tablespoon ground cinnamon

7 star anise, ground with a mortar and pestle

95 g (3½ oz/½ cup) soft brown sugar

Stir the apricot jam and sherry in a saucepan over medium heat until it becomes a sticky spread. Preheat the oven to 180°C (350°F/Gas 4). Prepare the ham by lifting off the skin but leaving the fat. Score the fat into diamonds about 2.5 cm (1 inch) deep. (This helps to open the ham up and get the flavour of the glaze into the meat.)

Mix the cinnamon with the star anise and rub into the fat. Spread two-thirds of the apricot glaze over the ham (keep the rest for basting). Press the brown sugar over the top, making sure some sugar gets into the score marks.

Put the ham in a roasting tin, add 2 cm (¾ inch) of water and cook for 1–1½ hours, basting with the remaining glaze from time to time. Be careful not to let the ham burn — check it every 20 minutes or so.

Serve with fennel coleslaw, your favourite chutney, mustard and crusty bread.

fennel coleslaw

¼ purple cabbage, cut into thin strips

¼ green cabbage, cut into thin strips

2 fennel bulbs, finely shaved

6 radishes, cut into thin rounds

2 long red chillies, deseeded and finely sliced

½ red onion, finely sliced

2 carrots, grated

juice of 1 lemon

4 tablespoons extra virgin olive oil

1 tablespoon seeded mustard

250 g (9 oz/1 cup) plain yoghurt or mayonnaise

2–3 large handfuls of herbs such as parsley, dill, basil, chives and tarragon, roughly chopped

Combine all the ingredients in a large bowl. Gently toss together and check the seasoning.

twice-cooked duck with figs

serves 4

Duck, Duck, Duck! Is there a better tasting bird out there? I doubt it very much. I could devote a whole chapter to my favourite game bird but I've just included this recipe that I cook at home — it doesn't have many ingredients but it's simply delicious. If figs are not in season use dried ones, or experiment with other fruit such as quince, orange, pear...

2 x 1.8 kg (4 lb) ducks

300 g (10½ oz) soft brown sugar

500 ml (17 fl oz/2 cups) veal stock

6 figs, cut into quarters

1 small handful of basil leaves

2½ tablespoons apple balsamic vinegar

2 tablespoons olive oil

200 g (7 oz) cavolo nero (or spinach or silverbeet)

juice of ½ lemon

Preheat the oven to 120°C (235°F/Gas ½). Rub the ducks with brown sugar, then slow-roast in the oven for 2½ hours. Let the ducks cool slightly, then cut them down to four breasts and four legs.

Meanwhile, put the veal stock in a pan and cook over medium heat until reduced by half.

Increase the oven to 160°C (315°F/Gas 2–3). Place the duck and stock in a roasting tin and cook for a further 10–15 minutes. Add the figs, basil and apple balsamic and season with salt and pepper, then cook for a further 5 minutes.

Heat the olive oil in a frying pan over medium heat and sauté the cavolo nero until wilted. Season with sea salt and cracked pepper and add the lemon juice. Serve with the duck and figs.

roasted brussels sprouts with chilli and speck

serves 4

As a child I hated brussels sprouts, probably more than any other food in the world. Looking back now, I don't think it was the sprouts I hated, it was how they were cooked (or should I say overcooked, until they turned soggy and grey). Now, if I'd been given them like this when I was eight years old (perhaps without the chilli) things might have been very different. I also like sprouts boiled until just tender, then tossed in a brown butter sauce with some chopped parsley and lemon. Brussels sprouts... definitely one of my favourite vegetables!

100 g (3½ oz) cubed speck or pancetta, cut into
largish pieces
20 brussels sprouts
2 tablespoons butter
a pinch of chilli flakes
zest of 1 lemon

Preheat the oven to 180°C (350°F/Gas 4). Put the speck in a roasting tin and cook for 10 minutes. Cut a deep cross in the bottom of each sprout so it cooks evenly and takes in the flavours.

Put the sprouts in the roasting tin with the speck. Add the butter and season with salt and pepper and roast for 20 minutes. Scatter with the chilli flakes and lemon zest to serve.

butter chicken with naan bread

serves 4

2 cm (¾ inch) piece of ginger, peeled and chopped

3 garlic cloves

2 tablespoons ground almonds

3 tablespoons bottled tandoori paste

250 g (9 oz/1 cup) Greek yoghurt

2 tablespoons oil or ghee

1 large onion, thinly sliced

750 g (1 lb 10 oz) chicken thigh fillets, halved

125 ml (4 fl oz/½ cup) chicken stock or water

1 small handful of coriander (cilantro) sprigs

steamed basmati rice, to serve

MINTED YOGHURT

125 g (4½ oz/½ cup) plain yoghurt

1 large handful of mint leaves, chopped

Preheat your grill and grease a ceramic baking dish with cooking oil spray.

Process the ginger, garlic, almonds, tandoori paste and yoghurt in a food processor until smooth.

Heat 1 tablespoon of the oil or ghee in a large deep frying pan and cook the onion for 5 minutes until soft. Tip into the dish.

Add ½ cupful of the tandoori mix to the chicken with a pinch of salt and turn to coat. Increase the heat under the frying pan and add the remaining oil. Add the chicken and cook for 5 minutes on each side. Add the remaining tandoori mix and stock and bring to the boil, then reduce the heat and simmer for 10 minutes. Stir in the coriander. Pour into the dish and grill for 3 minutes until bubbling.

To make the minted yoghurt, mix the yoghurt and mint together and serve with the butter chicken.

naan bread

1 free-range egg, lightly beaten

2 tablespoons oil or ghee

185 ml (6 fl oz/¾ cup) plain yoghurt

500 g (1 lb 2 oz/4 cups) plain (all-purpose) flour

2 teaspoons dried yeast

½ teaspoon baking powder

½ teaspoon salt

185 ml (6 fl oz/¾ cup) warmed milk

50 g (1¾ oz) butter, melted

Combine the egg, oil and yoghurt in a bowl.

Sift the flour into a large bowl, then add the yeast, baking powder and salt. Make a well in the centre and pour in the yoghurt mixture and the warmed milk. Mix to form a stiff dough.

Turn out the dough onto a floured surface and knead for 5 minutes, or until smooth and elastic. Place in a large oiled bowl, cover and leave in a warm place for 2 hours or until doubled in size.

Preheat your grill to high. Grease a baking tray and put it under the grill to heat up. Divide the dough into 10 portions and roll out two portions at time until 5 mm (¼ inch) thick. Stretch one end of the dough to make a teardrop shape. Place on the hot tray and grill for 1–2 minutes on each side until there are brown spots over the surface. Brush with melted butter and serve.

poldi's beef with bitter melon

serves 4

I know this book is called *'my' table* and is meant to have only my recipes in it, but I have to let you in on a secret — my mother-in-law, Poldi, cooks for me and the family at least once a week. She is a legend and one of the best cooks on the planet. This was the first dish she ever made for me and I was quite shocked when she put something on the table that I'd never even seen before: bitter melon. As I've now learnt, bitter melon (or bitter gourd) is mainly used in Asian cooking and is, as its name implies, one of the most bitter of all vegetables. It is held in high regard for its medicinal properties, and you'll probably need to buy it from your nearest Chinatown or an Asian grocer. It has quite a unique taste, but once you've acquired that taste this could become one of your favourite dishes.

1 bitter melon

2 tablespoons fermented black beans

6 garlic cloves, crushed or very finely chopped

1 tablespoon grated ginger

2 hot chillies, finely chopped

125 ml (4 fl oz/½ cup) light soy sauce

2 teaspoons sugar

400 g (14 oz) eye fillet of beef, cut into 5 mm
   (¼ inch) thick slices

cornflour

grapeseed or canola oil, for stir-frying

steamed rice, to serve

Cut the melon in half lengthways and remove the soft centre with a teaspoon. Without removing the skin, cut the melon into 5 mm (¼ inch) slices. Rinse and crush the black beans and mix with the garlic, ginger, chillies, soy sauce and sugar.

Toss the beef in a little cornflour to coat well.

Heat a little oil in a wok over high heat and stir-fry the meat in batches until browned and just cooked. Lift out onto a plate.

Add the melon to the wok with a touch of water and cook until just starting to soften (not too soft — you still want a bit of crunch to it). Remove from the wok.

Add the black bean sauce to the wok. Mix 1 teaspoon cornflour with 1 tablespoon water and add to the wok. Stir until the sauce thickens. Return the beef and bitter melon to the wok to heat through. Serve with steamed rice.

crumbed lamb cutlets with peperonata

serves 4

12 lamb cutlets (trimmed of fat, if you like)

160 g (5¾ oz/2 cups) fresh breadcrumbs (or
   cornflake crumbs)

2 tablespoons chopped rosemary

125 g (4½ oz/1 cup) plain (all-purpose) flour

2–3 free-range eggs, lightly beaten

grapeseed oil, for frying

1 lemon, cut into quarters

Season the lamb cutlets with salt and pepper.

Mix together the breadcrumbs and rosemary.

Coat each cutlet with flour, then shake off
any excess. Dip each cutlet into the egg to cover
completely, then drain off any excess. Dip each
cutlet into the rosemary breadcrumbs to coat
completely, patting the crumbs on firmly.

Heat some grapeseed oil in a frying pan over high
heat and pan-fry the cutlets until golden on each
side. (You can finish cooking in a 180°C/350°F/Gas 4
oven if you prefer your cutlets well done.)

Serve with lemon wedges and peperonata.

peperonata

2 red capsicums (peppers)

2 green capsicums (peppers)

250 ml (9 fl oz/1 cup) extra virgin olive oil

6 garlic cloves, finely sliced

2 red onions, cut into thin strips

1 bird's eye chilli, finely sliced

1 tablespoon tomato paste

2 large vine-ripened tomatoes

1 teaspoon sugar

2 tablespoons white or red wine vinegar

1 large handful of flat-leaf (Italian) parsley leaves

1 large handful of basil leaves

Hold the capsicums over an open flame or under a
hot grill until the skins are blackened and blistered.
Transfer to a bowl, cover with plastic wrap or a tea
towel and leave to steam so that the skin loosens.
After 20 minutes, peel and deseed the capsicums
and cut the flesh into long thin strips.

Heat 1 tablespoon of the oil in a saucepan and
ry the garlic over medium heat until softened. Add
the onion and cook until softened, then add the
chilli, tomato paste, tomatoes, sugar and vinegar
and cook for 1 minute. Add the capsicums, herbs, a
pinch of sea salt and the rest of the oil and cook for
10 minutes, then add in enough extra virgin olive oil
to make it luscious and moist.

eggplant parmigiana

serves 4

During the twenty short years I've worked as a chef, I've learned some lessons about food. The most important being that the simple things in life are often the best, and nowhere is this more true than with food. How many times have you eaten a beautiful ripe mango or a piece of cold watermelon on a hot summer day and thought 'what could be more perfect?', or caught a fish and cooked it simply with butter, lemon and parsley. I was once working with a world-famous chef, recreating his food for a huge event, and we had to substitute a vegetarian option for one of his courses. This eggplant parmigiana was what we offered, and we made quite a bit in case there was a horde of vegetarians. At the end of the night all the staff feasted on leftover parmigiana, and it was unanimously (although quietly!) agreed that everyone liked the simple eggplant parmigiana better than the world-famous chef's fancier dishes. So, please cook this and enjoy the simple things in life.

4 large eggplants (aubergines)
1 quantity of Italian tomato sauce (page 148)
200 g (7 oz) grated parmesan
500 g (1 lb 2 oz) Italian buffalo mozzarella, torn
    into pieces
2 handfuls of basil leaves
4 hard-boiled free-range eggs, peeled and sliced
200 ml (7 fl oz) olive oil

Preheat the oven to 200°C (400°F/Gas 6). Cut the eggplant into 2 cm (¾ inch) thick slices. Place on oiled baking trays, sprinkle with salt and bake for 20 minutes or until golden.

To put the parmigiana together you'll need to use half the tomato sauce — keep the rest for serving. Line a baking dish or loaf tin with baking paper, brush with oil and make layers, each time using a little of the eggplant, tomato sauce, parmesan, mozzarella and basil. Repeat until you have about five layers, using the egg in only the centre layer.

Lay a tray on top and weigh down (perhaps with a heavy ovenproof dish). Bake for 20 minutes at 160°C (315°F/Gas 2–3). Leave to cool with the weight still in place. When cool, turn out of the dish to slice. Reheat in the oven, if you like, and serve on hot Italian tomato sauce with more grated parmesan.

flathead with garlic, tomato and chunky bread

serves 4

3 tablespoons olive oil

8 garlic cloves, thinly sliced

1 tablespoon finely chopped long red chilli

4 anchovies

3 tablespoons chopped flat-leaf (Italian) parsley

400 g (14 oz) flathead fillets, cut into
   large pieces

500 g (1 lb 2 oz/2 cups) tinned tomatoes, crushed

125 ml (4 fl oz/½ cup) sparkling or plain water

2 thick slices of ciabbata, toasted and torn in pieces

In a cold saucepan, mix the oil, garlic, chilli and anchovies and then cook over medium heat until the garlic starts to turn golden. Add the parsley and flathead and cook for 30 seconds on each side.

Add the tomatoes and water and season to taste. Simmer until the flathead is just cooked through and season with salt and pepper. Add the bread and let it soak up the oil before serving.

silverbeet with garlic, lemon and olive oil

1 bunch of silverbeet or spinach

2 tablespoons olive oil

2 tablespoons butter

2 garlic cloves, thinly sliced

juice of 1 lemon

Remove the thick woody stems from the silverbeet and roughly chop. Heat the olive oil, butter and garlic in a frying pan over low heat until the garlic is soft. Add the silverbeet and cook until wilted. Season with salt and pepper, add the lemon juice and toss.

I was holding a cooking class for Tasting Australia in Adelaide (which has to be one of the best food festivals in Australia, hands down) and was intending to teach the students how to cook the best garlic prawns known to man. We had a little problem with the seafood for this event, so I went on the hunt in Adelaide to find some good fresh fish. I was advised to try Angelakis Brothers, and… let's just say that was great advice. Those guys know their seafood and have the very best of what South Australia has to offer. I ended up buying some sensational flathead and used it instead of the prawns — and the end result was as good, if not better, than what I'd been planning. The key to this story is to always use the freshest produce possible; if you can't find what you were hoping for, trust your instincts and you might just create a dish that's world class.

lobster with black bean and ginger

serves 4

I wanted to include a recipe for lobster that I think is a stand out — it really lets the lobster do what it does best and be a carrier of flavours. I always think Asian is the best preparation for lobster. This is a pretty simple dish, easy to eat and looks absolutely stunning when you present it to your guests. The sauce also works well with just about anything you can think of... tofu, prawns, crab, mussels, beef, chicken, pork and so on.

2–3 live lobsters

4 tablespoons fermented black beans

4 garlic cloves, finely chopped

3 teaspoons finely chopped ginger

2 teaspoons sugar

2 teaspoons sesame oil

125 ml (4 fl oz/½ cup) light soy sauce

2 tablespoons shaoxing rice wine or dry sherry

125 ml (4 fl oz/½ cup) chicken stock or water

2 tablespoons grapeseed oil

5 spring onions (scallions), green part only, chopped

1 large handful of coriander (cilantro) leaves

Put the lobsters in an ice slurry or in the freezer until they are immobile and asleep. Rinse and crush the black beans and mix with the garlic, ginger, sugar, sesame oil, soy sauce, shaoxing and chicken stock.

Using a tea towel in each hand, hold the head and the tail of the lobster. Twist firmly in opposite directions and pull apart. Remove the intestinal tract.

With a cleaver or chef's knife, cut the lobsters into 1–2 cm (½–¾ inch) medallions, leaving the shell on, and then cut the heads in half and remove the mustard (the stuff that looks the colour of mustard). Cut off the feelers and legs and lightly hit with the back of your knife to open the shell a bit, so it is easier to extract the meat later.

Heat the grapeseed oil in a wok until smoking and add the lobster medallions. Cook until the flesh turns white and the shells turn red, then add the feelers and legs and toss well. Add the black bean sauce and lobster mustard and toss together. Cover with a lid for a few minutes until cooked through. Sprinkle with spring onions and coriander leaves to serve.

master-stock pork belly with black vinegar dressing and cuttlefish salad

serves 4

This is the most complicated recipe in the book, but I'll be very proud if someone gives it a go. It's a restaurant dish that I have had on and off for many years at Hugo's and it's something that should be made when you really want to impress your guests or loved ones. The sweetness of the pork with the acidic salad is really a marriage made in heaven. You can use seared scallops, mud crab meat or prawns instead of the cuttlefish.

750 ml (26 fl oz/3 cups) vegetable oil or peanut oil

1 quantity of master-stock pork belly (opposite)

½ quantity of Chinese black vinegar sauce (opposite)

2 tablespoons roasted peanuts, crushed

CUTTLEFISH SALAD

100 g (3½ oz) cuttlefish, cleaned and sliced paper thin

1 long red chilli, thinly sliced

1 tablespoon thinly sliced ginger

1 handful of coriander (cilantro) leaves

8 mint leaves, torn

2 red Asian shallots, finely sliced

6 tablespoons diced pomelo or ruby grapefruit

½ quantity of nam jim dressing (page 30)

Fill a deep heavy-based saucepan or deep-fryer one-third full of oil and heat to (185°C/360°F). Deep-fry the pork belly, in batches, for a few minutes until golden and crisp, then drain on kitchen paper.

To make the cuttlefish salad, toss together the cuttlefish, chilli, ginger, coriander, mint, shallots and pomelo. Dress with the nam jim.

Heat the black vinegar sauce in a saucepan. Arrange the pork belly on a plate and pour the sauce over the pork. Top with the cuttlefish salad and sprinkle with roasted peanuts.

master-stock pork belly

250 ml (9 fl oz/1 cup) soy sauce

250 ml (9 fl oz/1 cup) shoaxing rice wine (or
   dry sherry)

115 g (4 oz/½ cup) crushed yellow rock sugar

1 large knob of ginger, sliced

3 garlic cloves, sliced

4 star anise

2 cinnamon sticks

3 pieces of dried tangerine peel

1 x 400 g (14 oz) boneless piece of pork belly

Put everything except the pork belly in a large
pan with 1.5 litres (6 cups) of water and bring to
the boil. Add the pork belly, bring back to the boil,
then reduce the heat and simmer, uncovered, for
1½ hours.

Remove from the heat, put a lid on the pan and
leave the pork to cook in the stock. Once cool, lift
out the pork and place on a tray with another tray on
top with a weight on it to press the pork belly.
Refrigerate overnight, then cut into 2 cm (¾ inch)
thick slices. You can strain the master stock, reboil
it, let it cool and then store in the freezer until
next time.

chinese black vinegar sauce

1 tablespoon vegetable oil

2 garlic cloves, finely chopped

2 tablespoons chopped red Asian shallots

3 tablespoons finely sliced ginger

3 tablespoons light soy sauce

125 ml (4 fl oz/½ cup) Chinese black vinegar

120 g (4 oz) grated palm sugar

2 tablespoons fish sauce

Heat the oil in a saucepan over medium heat and
cook the garlic and shallots until golden. Add the
ginger, soy and vinegar and some salt and pepper,
then reduce the heat and simmer for 10 minutes.

Stir in the sugar, increase the heat a little and cook
for 10 minutes. Stir in the fish sauce.

moroccan tagine of spatchcock with preserved lemon and herb couscous

serves 4

CHERMOULA — WET MIX

1 large handful of coriander (cilantro), chopped

1 large handful of parsley, chopped

1 large handful of mint, chopped

3 garlic cloves, chopped

2 teaspoons ground cumin

2 teaspoons ground coriander

1 teaspoon paprika

1 small red chilli, chopped

3 tablespoons lemon juice

4 tablespoons olive oil

4 spatchcocks (poussins), quartered

2 tablespoons olive oil

2 onions, sliced

1 teaspoon ground ginger

500 g (1 lb 2 oz) desiree potatoes, peeled and cut into thick wedges

1 teaspoon saffron threads

125 ml (4 fl oz/½ cup) hot chicken stock

zest of 1 large preserved lemon, sliced

16 dates, seeds removed

20 whole green olives

185 g (6 oz/1 cup) couscous

250 ml (9 fl oz/1 cup) boiling chicken stock

1 tablespoon butter

2 tablespoons finely chopped mixed fresh herbs (coriander, mint, parsley)

To make the chermoula, mix the herbs, garlic, spices, chilli and lemon juice in a food processor. While the motor is still running, drizzle in the oil and process until smooth. Season with salt and pepper.

Spoon the chermoula over the spatchcock pieces and toss to coat evenly. Cover and marinate for 4 hours or overnight.

Heat a large frying pan over medium–high heat. Lift the spatchcock out of its marinade (keeping the marinade) and cook for 2–3 minutes until browned.

Heat the oil in the tagine base over a low flame. Add the onions and ginger and cook for 4–5 minutes until softened but not coloured.

Place the spatchcock over the onions and add the rest of the marinade. Place the potato wedges around the spatchcock. Stir the saffron into the hot stock and pour over the chicken. Scatter with the preserved lemon, dates and green olives. Cover and cook for 45 minutes to 1 hour until the spatchcock is cooked through and the juices run clear.

Meanwhile, put the couscous in a bowl, pour in the hot chicken stock, add the butter and leave to sit for 10 minutes. Break up the couscous with a fork and toss with the chopped herbs. Season with salt and pepper and serve with the tagine.

A tagine makes a wonderful gift for someone who loves to cook. They aren't expensive and having one in your kitchen (where you can readily see it) encourages you to use it. The tagine (the name belongs to both the dish and its cooking pot) originated in Morocco and is basically a stew of meat coated in spices and slowly cooked in the ceramic pot. The pots are designed so that the steam rises to the top of the tagine, then trickles back down into the sauce to create a wonderfully flavoursome and moist stew — great for less expensive cuts of meat. My favourite tagines are lamb shoulder, chicken, seafood and even a vegetarian version with pumpkin and eggplant.

confit of ocean trout with pea purée, braised fennel and pernod sauce

serves 4

It is hard to believe that rainbow trout and ocean trout are actually the same fish, just reared at different altitudes and in different waters. The rainbow trout is a freshwater fish and the ocean trout is saltwater and, of course, grows to a much larger size. The cooking technique I use here works with most fish and is a real joy to do — the fish is roasted slowly in olive oil, sealing in all its precious flavour and texture. The pernod and orange sauce cuts through the richness of the fish, and the peas and guanciale just finish it off to perfection.

350 ml (12 fl oz) olive oil

4 baby fennel bulbs

500 ml (17 fl oz/2 cups) orange juice

4 tablespoons pernod or vodka

1 star anise

1 cinnamon stick

4 x 100 g (3½ oz) ocean trout fillets (or Atlantic salmon), at room temperature

2 tablespoons butter

200 g (7 oz) frozen peas

40 g (1½ oz) guanciale or pancetta, diced

2 tablespoons salmon caviar (if you like)

Preheat the oven to 65°C (150°F/Gas ¼). Pour the olive oil into a baking dish and place in the oven.

Put the fennel in a saucepan with the orange juice, pernod, star anise and cinnamon. Bring to a simmer and cook until just tender. Lift out the fennel and reserve the cooking liquid for later.

Season the trout with salt and pepper. Place in the baking dish with the oil and cook in the oven for 10 minutes, or until cooked medium–rare.

Heat the reserved fennel cooking liquid in a frying pan over medium heat and cook until thickened to a sauce consistency. Add 1 tablespoon of the butter and season with salt and pepper.

Bring 500 ml (17 fl oz/2 cups) of water and a pinch of salt to the boil in a saucepan. Add the peas and cook for 1 minute, then strain and refresh under cold water. Blend the peas with the other tablespoon of butter and season to taste.

Meanwhile, heat a touch of oil in a frying pan over medium heat and fry the guanciale until crisp.

Gently heat the pea purée and spoon onto the plates. Place the trout on the pea purée. Spoon the sauce around the trout, sprinkle the guanciale into the sauce and serve with the fennel. Garnish with salmon caviar, if you like.

NOTE You can keep the oil from the fish. Keep it in the fridge for dressing a salad or pasta.

pot-roasted chicken with tarragon gravy

serves 4

If you are looking for a different way with roast chicken, then look no further. This one is cooked in a 'pot' with some beautiful ingredients that permeate the whole bird, so the meat is wonderfully succulent. The glossy gravy that is made from the pan juices has tarragon leaves added and is really sublime. This is a very simple dish to cook, and I love to serve it with the cauliflower and taleggio, or with crisp croutons smothered with soft goat's cheese and flavoured with a hint of lemon and chilli.

1 x 2 kg (5 lb) free-range chicken

1 tablespoon butter

1 whole garlic bulb, halved

2 leeks, chopped into 3 cm (1¼ inch) pieces

2 carrots, chopped into 3 cm (1¼ inch) pieces

20 shiitake mushrooms (or other mushrooms if you like)

2 tablespoons olive oil

375 ml (13 fl oz/1½ cups) dry white wine

500 ml (17 fl oz/2 cups) hot chicken stock

leaves from 1 bunch of tarragon

Preheat the oven to 220°C (425°F/Gas 7). Turn the wings under the chicken and truss for roasting. Rub the chicken with the butter and garlic, then season.

Place the leeks, carrots, mushrooms and garlic in a casserole dish. Place the chicken on top of the vegetables, drizzle with olive oil and then pour the wine around the chicken (not over the top).

Roast for 30 minutes, then pour the hot chicken stock around the chicken. Reduce the oven to 180°C (350°F/Gas 4), cover with a lid and roast for another 30–45 minutes.

Lift out the chicken and vegetables (keep covered and warm) and strain the pan juices into a saucepan. Simmer over medium heat until reduced and thickened to make a glossy gravy. Add the tarragon leaves and check the seasoning just before serving with the chicken and vegetables.

cauliflower with bacon, taleggio and breadcrumbs

serves 4

1 cauliflower, cut into florets

1 onion, finely chopped

100 g (3½ oz) pancetta or bacon, finely chopped

2 tablespoons chopped parsley

40 g (1½ oz) butter

40 g (1½ oz) plain (all-purpose) flour

425 ml (15 fl oz/1¾ cups) milk

100 g (3½ oz) taleggio, broken into pieces

a pinch of nutmeg

1 teaspoon dijon mustard

25 g (1 oz/¼ cup) grated parmesan

25 g (1 oz/⅓ cup) fresh breadcrumbs

Bring a large saucepan of salted water to the boil, add the cauliflower and cook for 4 minutes or until just tender. Drain and place the cauliflower in a greased ceramic baking dish.

Meanwhile, heat a frying pan over medium heat and add the onion and pancetta. Cook for 3–4 minutes until just starting to change colour, then add the parsley. Spoon over the cauliflower.

Preheat the oven to 180°C (350°F/Gas 4). Melt the butter in a saucepan over medium heat. Stir in the flour and cook over low heat, stirring continuously. Gradually add the milk, stirring all the time, and bring to the boil. Add the taleggio and stir until melted. Season and add the nutmeg, mustard and half the parmesan, then stir until melted.

Pour the sauce over the cauliflower. Sprinkle with the remaining parmesan and the breadcrumbs. Bake for 15 minutes or until golden.

steamed coral trout with soy, mirin, crispy garlic and chilli

serves 4

Of all the recipes I cook at home, this is the one I would make for my last supper. It has everything I love about food in one dish: firstly, it's a whole fish (and I like nothing better than being presented with a whole fish); secondly, it is Asian in flavour, but not too overpowering (and I'm sure I have Asian blood running through my veins somewhere); thirdly, would have to be the texture of the different components and the way they all work together to bring a party to the mouth. And I guess the fourth reason I love this, is that I've just spent a glorious day on a reef in the tropics catching these amazing creatures. That's enough to put a huge smile on my face.

1 x 1.5 kg (3 lb 5 oz) coral trout, scaled and gutted

125 ml (4 fl oz/½ cup) shaoxing rice wine (or dry sherry)

125 ml (4 fl oz/½ cup) light soy sauce

6 spring onions (scallions), julienned (keep the white and green parts separate — the green part in cold water in the fridge)

3 tablespoons julienned ginger

250–500 ml (9–17 fl oz/1–2 cups) peanut oil

4 garlic cloves, finely sliced

2 long red chillies, finely sliced

4 tablespoons chilli sauce

1 handful of coriander (cilantro) leaves

8 lime wedges

steamed rice, to serve

Preheat the oven to 180°C (350°F/Gas 4). Make three incisions through the skin into the flesh on both sides of the fish and then put the fish in a baking tin.

Mix together the shaoxing and soy sauce and pour over the fish. Sprinkle the white julienned spring onion and ginger over the fish, cover and cook for 15 minutes or until the flesh is cooked through but still moist.

Meanwhile, heat the peanut oil in a saucepan and cook the garlic and chillies over medium–high heat until golden and crispy. Drain on kitchen paper.

Drizzle the chilli sauce over the fish, top with the coriander and green spring onions and scatter with the crispy garlic and chillies. Serve with lime wedges, rice, Asian greens and a cold Asian beer.

affogato

serves 1

freshly ground coffee
1 scoop of vanilla ice cream
1½ tablespoons frangelico liqueur

Use an electric coffee machine, plunger or Italian coffee maker to make 3 tablespoons of hot strong espresso. Pour into a shot glass. Pour the liqueur into another shot glass.

Place a scoop of ice cream into a glass or bowl. Arrange on a serving plate with the coffee and liqueur on the side. When ready to eat, pour the hot coffee and liqueur over the ice cream.

vanilla ice cream

450 ml (16 fl oz) milk
450 ml (16 fl oz) cream
125 g (4½ oz) glucose
3 vanilla pods
125 g (4½ oz) sugar
12 free-range egg yolks

Stir the milk, cream and glucose in a saucepan over medium–low heat. Split the vanilla pods lengthways and scrape the seeds into the pan. Bring to a simmer.

Whisk the sugar into the egg yolks in a large bowl. Pour half the hot milk over the egg yolks, whisking all the time. Then pour the whole lot back into the saucepan. Stir constantly with a rubber spatula over low heat until the mixture thickens enought to coat the spatula.

Pass through a fine strainer and cool in the fridge. Once cool, churn in an ice-cream machine, following the manufacturer's instructions, or put in the freezer and whisk every 15–30 minutes.

gorgonzola dolce latte with truffled honey and toasted sourdough

serves 4

16 thin slices of sourdough
200 g (7 oz) gorgonzola dolce latte or other
    blue cheese such as roquefort
2 tablespoons truffled honey or other honey
1 bunch of dried or fresh muscatel grapes
    or fresh figs

Place the cheese on a platter and allow to come to room temperature. Preheat the oven to 180°C (350°F/Gas 4). Put the bread on a baking tray and bake until crisp and light golden.

Heat the honey slightly so that it becomes runny and then drizzle over the cheese. Serve with the bread and fruit.

churros with hot chocolate sauce

makes about 25–30 churros

These would have to be the most indulgent and addictive dessert on the face of the planet — so good they should probably have a government health warning. The funny thing is that in Spain these are actually eaten for breakfast, in the same way that the French eat *pain au chocolate* (something else I can't get my head around). These are easy to make — just make sure the oil for deep-frying is fresh and you haven't cooked spring rolls or salt and pepper squid in there, otherwise you'll get some pretty strange flavours lurking in your doughnuts. Traditionally these are dusted with plain sugar but I like to add a little cinnamon. Enjoy.

CHOCOLATE SAUCE
200 ml (7 fl oz) cream
200 g (7 oz) dark chocolate, roughly chopped

CINNAMON SUGAR
55 g (2 oz/¼ cup) sugar
1 teaspoon ground cinnamon

vegetable oil, for deep-frying
2 tablespoons soft brown sugar
½ teaspoon salt
70 g (2½ oz/⅓ cup) butter, softened
125 g (4½ oz/1 cup) plain (all-purpose) flour
2 free-range eggs
½ teaspoon vanilla extract

To make the chocolate sauce, heat the cream in a saucepan over medium heat until hot. Put the chocolate in a bowl, pour in the hot cream and mix until smooth. Keep warm until needed.

To make the cinnamon sugar, mix the sugar and cinnamon together and set aside.

Fill a large deep frying pan one-third full of vegetable oil and heat to 180°C (350°F).

Combine the brown sugar, salt, butter and 250 ml (9 fl oz/1 cup) of water in a saucepan over medium heat. Bring to the boil, then remove from the heat and stir in the flour. Whisk together the eggs and vanilla, add to the pan and stir well.

Attach a large star nozzle to your piping bag and fill the bag with the churros dough.

Test your oil by squeezing a small amount of dough into it. The dough should bubble up right away or the oil is not hot enough.

Once the oil is hot, squeeze 10 cm (4 inch) lengths of dough into the oil. You should be able to cook four or five churros at a time. Cook for about 2 minutes, then turn with a slotted spoon. Cook for another 2–3 minutes until golden brown. Remove with a slotted spoon and drain on kitchen paper.

While still warm, roll the churros in the cinnamon sugar, then serve with hot chocolate sauce.

chocolate and sticky date pudding with butterscotch sauce and red wine strawberries

serves 8–10

BUTTERSCOTCH SAUCE

300 g (10½ oz) soft brown sugar

150 g (5½ oz) butter

150 ml (5 fl oz) cream

300 g (10½ oz) pitted dates, cut in half

2 teaspoons bicarbonate of soda

600 ml (21 fl oz) boiling water

200 g (7 oz) soft brown sugar

120 g (4 oz) unsalted butter

1 vanilla pod, split in half lengthways and
    seeds scraped out

2 free-range eggs

460 g (1 lb) plain (all-purpose) flour

3 teaspoons baking powder

300 g (10½ oz) chocolate buttons

thick cream, to serve

RED WINE STRAWBERRIES

115 g (4 oz/½ cup) sugar

250 ml (9 fl oz/1 cup) pinot noir

1 cinnamon stick

1 punnet of strawberries, hulled and halved

To make the butterscotch sauce, combine the brown sugar, butter and cream in a pan over medium heat. Bring to the boil, stirring, then simmer for 5 minutes. Line a 25 cm (10 inch) springform cake tin with greased foil. Pour in half of the butterscotch sauce (keep the rest for serving).

Mix the dates and bicarbonate of soda in a small bowl. Pour in the boiling water and leave to cool. Preheat the oven to 180°C (350°F/Gas 4).

Beat the sugar, butter and vanilla seeds in a bowl until creamy. Add in the eggs and beat well. Mix in the date mixture. Sift together the flour and baking powder and add to the bowl. Stir in the chocolate.

Pour into the tin and bake for 30 minutes, then reduce the heat to 160°C (315°F/Gas 2–3) and cook for another hour. Test with a skewer, then remove from the oven and cool in the tin before turning out.

Meanwhile, to make the red wine strawberries, mix the sugar with 3 tablespoons of water in a pan to form a paste. Heat until it turns light caramel, then add the red wine (be careful; it will spit) and stir. Add the cinnamon and cook for 10 minutes. Pour over the strawberries and leave to macerate for up to an hour before serving.

Cut the pudding into slices and pour the butterscotch sauce over the top. If necessary, heat in the microwave until warm and serve with cream and red wine strawberries.

zabaglione with soaked strawberries

serves 4

I learned to make zabaglione a little less than twenty years ago at a place called Mario's in Fitzroy, Melbourne. I couldn't believe how simple this dessert was and how cheap it was to make. This was the dish that taught me all about temperature and the need to be in control of the heat… because the last thing you want to end up with here is a panful of scrambled eggs. The key is to whisk the egg yolks, sugar and alcohol as fast as you can, to get as much air into the mixture as possible. The end result should be light and fluffy — it will take about five minutes of whisking, and your arm will probably be pretty sore by the end of it, but it is very rewarding. I love to serve this with macerated berries, and sponge finger biscuits to scoop up the zabaglione.

SOAKED STRAWBERRIES

1 punnet of strawberries, hulled and halved

125 ml (4 fl oz/½ cup) vin santo or other dessert wine

125 ml (4 fl oz/½ cup) honey

3 tablespoons sugar

ZABAGLIONE

8 egg yolks

170 ml (5½ fl oz/⅔ cup) vin santo or other dessert wine

1 tablespoon aged balsamic vinegar

230 g (8 oz/⅓ cup) caster (superfine) sugar

Italian sponge finger biscuits

icing (confectioners') sugar, for dusting

Put the strawberries in a heatproof bowl. Mix the vin santo, honey and sugar in a small pan over medium heat until the sugar dissolves. Pour over the strawberries and leave for 10 minutes, then drain the liquid into another container to use later.

To make the zabaglione, set a stainless steel mixing bowl over a saucepan of barely simmering water. Place the egg yolks, vin santo, balsamic vinegar and sugar in the bowl and whisk for about 5–10 minutes until light and fluffy. Be careful that the water doesn't boil too fast or the eggs will scramble. You can take the bowl off the heat for 10 seconds if it gets too hot (keep whisking!) and then put it back, turning down the heat in the process. (Use a tea towel to hold the bowl — it can get a bit warm.)

Serve the zabaglione with the strawberries and a little of the macerating liquid. I like to use Italian sponge finger biscuits dusted with icing sugar for scooping up the zabaglione.

fig and vanilla margarita

makes 4

The margarita stems from the 1930s, when an actress called Marjorie King was a guest at Rancha La Gloria. The owner, Danny Herrera, made her a tequila cocktail because she was allergic to every other spirit. He named his creation in her memory.

VANILLA SYRUP
100 g (3½ oz) sugar
1 vanilla bean, split lengthways and seeds
    scraped out

4 whole fresh figs
185 ml (6 fl oz/¾ cup) Silver Tequila
60 ml (2 fl oz/¼ cup) Massenez Pomme Verte
    (green apple liqueur)
60 ml (2 fl oz/¼ cup) fresh lime juice
2 tablespoons vanilla syrup

To make the vanilla syrup, put the sugar and 100 ml (3½ fl oz) of water in a pan over medium heat and simmer until the sugar has dissolved. Add the vanilla bean and seeds and simmer until fragrant. Leave to cool, then strain.

   Muddle the figs in a Boston shaker, then add all the other ingredients. Fill with ice, shake well and double strain into chilled martini glasses.

mr hendrix

makes 4

My friend, Mark Ward, who is two parts English to one part Aussie, created this drink for the Australasian launch of Hendrick's Gin. Hendrick's gin is made with cucumber and rose petals, so it's really light, refreshing and floral — just perfect for sitting in the garden and drinking with cucumber sandwiches. (Oh Mark, how English! Even better, I think, would be the spicy banana flower salad.)

zest of 4 limes
8 kaffir lime leaves, plus some to serve
200 ml (7 fl oz) Hendrick's gin
60 ml (2 fl oz/¼ cup) Massenez Pomme Verte
    (green apple liqueur)
2 tablespoons Cinzano Bianco
1 tablespoon elderflower cordial
ice

Put the lime zest into four martini glasses. Tear and press the kaffir lime leaves into a mixing glass, then add all the other ingredients. Fill with ice and stir until the glass is frosted. Strain into the chilled martini glasses and garnish with a kaffir lime leaf.

lady houghton

makes 4

My good mate, Deb Houghton, is a bloody legend: good-looking, huge heart, infectious laugh, and she can out-last all the boys like the good country girl she is. We celebrated a special birthday for her a couple of years back and our head mixologist, Mark Ward, created a special drink in honour of the gorgeous Miss Houghton. Just like our Deb, it's absolutely delicious.

185 ml (6 fl oz/¾ cup) 42 Below passionfruit vodka
60 ml (2 fl oz/¼ cup) Massenez Crème de Peche
60 ml (2 fl oz/¼ cup) lemon juice
12 dashes of peach bitters
20 ml (1 fl oz) egg white
20 ml (1 fl oz) sugar syrup
dried peach, to serve

Put all the ingredients into a Boston shaker filled with ice and shake well. Double strain into a glass and garnish with a dried piece of peach, if you like.

espresso martini

makes 4

This is a great cocktail to serve with dessert, after dessert or just as dessert. It brings together the traditional digestif elements of coffee and cognac. Have one of these and a nice large chunk of dark chocolate and the heavens will be shining down on you.

ORANGE AND VANILLA SYRUP
100 g (3½ oz) sugar
zest of 1 orange
1 vanilla bean, split lengthways and seeds
    scraped out

185 ml (6 fl oz/¾ cup) cognac
20 ml (1 fl oz) coffee liqueur
120 ml (4 fl oz/½ cup) fresh espresso
ice
grated dark chocolate, to serve

To make the orange and vanilla syrup, stir the sugar and 100 ml (3½ fl oz) of water in a saucepan over medium heat until dissolved. Add the orange zest and vanilla bean and seeds and simmer until fragrant. Leave to cool, then strain. You need 2 tablespoons for this cocktail so keep the rest in a clean container.

Add the cognac, coffee liqueur, orange and vanilla syrup and espresso to a Boston shaker and fill with ice. Shake well, then strain into martini glasses. Garnish with grated chocolate to serve.

mango daiquiri

makes 4

The original daiquiri was made with white rum, lime and sugar syrup, however, since Hugo's opened its doors, this mango variation has outsold most of our other cocktails. It's a perfect holiday brunch drink, if you're sitting on a balcony overlooking the beach, or enjoy it at sunset with some spicy prawns from the barbecue. You can change the mango to peach, mixed berries or guava.

180 ml (6 fl oz) Bacardi Superior rum
60 ml (2 fl oz/¼ cup) mango liqueur
120 ml (4 fl oz/½ cup) mango purée
2 tablespoons fresh lime juice
1 tablespoon sugar syrup (page 108)
crushed ice
mixed berries, to serve (if you like)

Blend together the rum, mango liqueur and purée, lime juice and sugar syrup, then add 1 large scoop of crushed ice and blend until smooth. Put some berries in the bottom of each glass and pour the daiquiri over to serve.

index

THIS BOOK IS DEDICATED TO MY MUM, JOY, FOR MAKING "MY TABLE", AS A KID GROWING
UP, ALWAYS AN ENJOYABLE TIME!

Published in 2008 by Murdoch Books Pty Limited

Murdoch Books Australia
Pier 8/9, 23 Hickson Road
Millers Point NSW 2000
Phone: +61 (0) 2 8220 2000
Fax: +61 (0) 2 8220 2558
www.murdochbooks.com.au

Murdoch Books UK Limited
Erico House, 6th Floor
93–99 Upper Richmond Road
Putney, London SW15 2TG
Phone: +44 (0) 20 8785 5995
Fax: +44 (0) 20 8785 5985
www.murdochbooks.co.uk

Chief Executive: Juliet Rogers
Publishing Director: Kay Scarlett

Project Manager: Jane Price
Editor: Gordana Trifunovic
Food editor: Sonia Greig
Photography: Anson Smart
Stylist: David Morgan
Production: Monique Layt
Colour separation: Splitting Image Colour Studio

Printed by 1010 Printing International Ltd in 2008. PRINTED IN CHINA.

National Library of Australia Cataloguing-in-Publication Data

Evans, Peter Daryl, 1973–. My table: food for entertaining / Pete Evans.
ISBN 97181741962406 (pbk.) Includes index.
Entertaining. Cookery. 641.568

The publisher and stylist would like to thank the following:
Kris Coad and Sam Robinson for their amazing ceramics used throughout the book; Top3 by Design, Bondi Junction;
Ici et La; Porters Paints; The Bay Tree, Woollahra.

And, particularly, Tony and Suzanne Annand and family for the generous use of their house for photography.

IMPORTANT: Those who might be at risk from the effects of salmonella poisoning (the elderly, pregnant women,
young children and those suffering from immune deficiency diseases) should consult their doctor with any
concerns about eating raw eggs.
OVEN GUIDE: You may find cooking times vary depending on the oven you are using. For fan-forced ovens, as a
general rule, set the oven temperature to 20°C (35°F) lower than indicated in the recipe.